BEST PRACTICES *in Action*

Fluency Practice
Read-Aloud Plays

GRADES 5–6

BY KATHLEEN M. HOLLENBECK

NEW YORK • TORONTO • LONDON • AUCKLAND • SYDNEY
MEXICO CITY • NEW DELHI • HONG KONG • BUENOS AIRES

Teaching Resources

To the patient

and dedicated teachers

who guide

and encourage students

on the path toward fluency.

Cover design by Brian LaRossa
Interior design by Kathy Massaro
Interior art by Delana Bettoli, Mike Gordon, and Mike Moran

ISBN–13: 978-0-439-55421-3
ISBN–10: 0-439-55421-7

Copyright © 2006 by Kathleen M. Hollenbeck
All rights reserved. Published by Scholastic Inc.
Printed in the U.S.A.

4   5   6   7   8   9   10   40   14   13   12

Contents

INTRODUCTION

*f*luency, the ability to decode words quickly and accurately, is more than just a buzzword in education. It is a fundamental skill that must be achieved in order for readers to find meaning in words.

Oral reading offers tremendous insight into a student's level of fluency. The fluent reader glides through text almost effortlessly, reading with meaning, expression, and appropriate pacing. A struggling reader labors over words, deciphering them in a slow, halting manner that hinders comprehension.

Training and practice are essential to achieving reading fluency, and oral reading offers an unmatched opportunity for both. *Read-Aloud Plays for Building Fluency: Grades 5–6* includes 14 oral reading opportunities that make reading practice easy, entertaining, and rewarding. The plays explore topics from core-curricular areas and adhere to national standards for fifth and sixth grades.

In addition to the plays, inside this book you'll find activities to strengthen skills in fluency, phonics, and oral reading, a section devoted to enhancing the Readers Theater experience (see Using Readers Theater, page 14); and tools for assessment, including a teacher rubric and a checklist students can use to guide and monitor their own reading progress (see Assessing Fluency, page 8). The plays and activities target specific skills designed to increase word recognition, decoding accuracy, use of expression, and ultimately, comprehension—the primary goal of reading instruction.

The text of each play has been leveled using readability scores from the Lexile Framework for Reading (see chart, page 13). These scores offer guidelines to help you select the scripts that best match the needs and reading levels of each student. The plays are ready for use to practice, strengthen, and assess skills in reading fluency. And they all share the same objective: to give students practice reading comfortably, confidently, and with enthusiasm, helping to build an ever-growing flock of fluent readers within the walls of your classroom.

Fluency: An Overview

What Is Fluency?

Fluency is the mark of a proficient reader. When a student reads text quickly, gets most of the words right, and uses appropriate expression and phrasing, we say that he or she has achieved fluency. Fluency frees readers from the struggle that slows them down. Hence, they are able to read for meaning and to understand. They can attend to the details of text, pausing as indicated and varying tone and pace to enhance comprehension for both themselves and potential listeners.

How Does Fluency Develop?

As with every skill worth developing, fluency sharpens with experience. Exposure to print, immersion in a rich linguistic environment, and practice, practice, practice all lead to fluent reading.

From the emergent on up, readers must learn and apply tools to help them advance. The National Institute for Literacy (NIFL) speaks of fluency as a skill in flux.

> "Fluency is not a stage of development at which readers can read all words quickly and easily. Fluency changes, depending on what readers are reading, their familiarity with the words, and the amount of their practice with reading text. Even very skilled readers may read in a slow, labored manner when reading texts with many unfamiliar words or topics." (NIFL, 2001)

Readers are most comfortable (and most fluent) when reading what they have seen before or what they know most about. When venturing beyond these areas, they must rely on word attack skills, prior knowledge, and the host of tools that have helped them advance to this point.

Ways to Build Fluency

* **MODEL FLUENT READING.** Do an interactive read-aloud. As you read, model (and point out) aspects of fluent reading such as phrasing, pacing, and expression. Help students understand that people aren't born knowing how do this; they learn it by hearing it and trying it themselves. Also ask open-ended questions before, during, and after the reading, soliciting students' prior knowledge and extending their understanding, comprehension, and connection with the topic. This connection can advance student interaction with the text and promote optimal conditions for fluency.

"Fluent readers read aloud effortlessly and with expression. Their reading sounds natural, as if they are speaking. Readers who have not yet developed fluency read slowly, word by word. Their oral reading is choppy and plodding."

NATIONAL INSTITUTE FOR LITERACY, 2001

"Students who practise (sic) by spending time with books that provide just enough challenge will become better readers. Students who practise (sic) by spending time with books that are too hard are not likely to increase the power of their reading."

(CHARLTON, 2005)

PROVIDE STUDENTS WITH PLENTY OF READING PRACTICE. Oral reading is highly effective for tracking and strengthening fluency. It enables both the reader and the listener to hear the reader and assess progress, and it allows the listener to provide guidance as needed. Encourage reading practice with any of the following:

- **Repeated Reading:** Read aloud while a student listens. Then read again while the student follows along. Finally, have the student read the same text aloud alone. This technique is most helpful for struggling readers.

- **Paired Repeated Reading:** Group students in pairs, matching above-level readers with on-level readers and on-level readers with those below level. Encourage partners to take turns reading aloud to each other, each reading a short passage three times and then getting feedback. This manner of grouping provides every struggling reader with a more proficient reader to model.

- **Readers Theater:** Students work in groups to rehearse and perform one or more plays from this book. See Using Readers Theater, page 14, for more.

SELECT APPROPRIATE TEXT. To develop fluency, a student must practice reading text at his or her independent reading level—the level at which he or she is able to accurately decode 96 to 100 percent of the words in a given text. This level varies for every student. By assessing each student's reading level up front, you will be prepared to select appropriate texts and ensure that your students get a lot of practice reading at a level at which they achieve success (Rasinski, 2003; Worthy and Broaddus, 2001/2002). For information about how to use text to assess fluency, see Assessing Fluency, page 8.

GIVE ROOM TO GROW. To help a student advance in fluency, present text at his or her instructional level. This text can be read with 90 to 95 percent accuracy. With a little help, the student can get almost all the words right (Blevins, 2001; Rasinski, 2003).

PROVIDE DIRECT INSTRUCTION AND FEEDBACK. Prepare students before they read. First review phonics skills they will need to decode words. Draw attention to sight words, root words, affixes, and word chunks. Preteach difficult or unfamiliar words. Demonstrate the use of intonation, phrasing, and expression, and tell students when they have done these well. Listen to students read, and offer praise as well as helpful tips for the next attempt.

✳ HIGHLIGHT PHRASING.

One of the most effective ways to help students who are struggling with fluency is to use phrase-cued text. Phrase-cued text is marked by slashes to indicate where readers should pause. One slash indicates a pause or meaningful chunk of text within a sentence. Two slashes indicates a longer pause at the end of a sentence. Ready-made samples of phrase-cued text are available (see Resources for Reading Fluency, Comprehension, and Readers Theater, page 15), but you can also convert any passage of text to phrase-cued text by reading it aloud, listening for pauses and meaningful chunks of text, and drawing slashes in the appropriate places. (See the example, above, from the play "The Pied Piper," page 39.) Model fluent reading with proper phrasing and invite students to practice with the text you have marked.

> **Julie:** The rats/ are too numerous,/ Mayor,/ and/ they are enormous!// Even/ our cats and dogs/ are afraid of them,/ so fierce/ and so numerous/ are these rats!// We must stop/ the rodents/ from taking over/ our town.// What are you /going to do?//

Where Does Vocabulary Fit In?

Stumbling over words constitutes one of the main setbacks on the way to fluency. It remains in your students' best interest, then, to grow familiar with words they will likely encounter in reading. Cunningham and Allington (2003) urge active use of word walls, inviting student participation in choosing words to put on the walls, eliminating words rarely used, and reviewing the list words daily.

Enhancing Comprehension

In all reading instruction, it is important to remember that reading imparts meaning, and so the fundamental goal of reading is to comprehend. All other instruction—phonics, phonemic awareness, auditory discrimination—is wasted effort if comprehension gets lost in the process. Consequently, those who find no purpose or meaning in the written word will soon lose interest in reading it altogether.

Avoid this by teaching your students strategies to enhance comprehension. Help them learn to question the text they are reading. *What is the message? Does it make sense to them? Do they know what it means?* Find out by asking questions. Ask questions before students read, to prepare them for the play. Ask as they read, to deepen their understanding of the text. Ask additional questions after they read, to clear up any comprehension issues and summarize the play. Teach your students to formulate questions of their own to give them a vested interest in what they are reading.

> "Students who are having trouble with comprehension may not be putting words together in meaningful phrases or chunks as they read. Their oral reading is characterized by a choppy, word-by-word delivery that impedes comprehension. These students need instruction in phrasing written text into appropriate segments."
>
> (BLEVINS, 2001)

Assessing Fluency

There are two ways to assess a student's progress in fluency: informally and formally. Informal assessment involves listening to students read aloud, noting how easily, quickly, and accurately they read, and deciding how well they attend to phrasing, expression, and other elements. Formal assessment involves timing a student's oral reading to create a tangible record of his or her progress throughout the school year.

To conduct an informal assessment of students' reading fluency, use the reproducible Teacher Rubric for Oral Reading Fluency on page 9. Have a student read aloud for five to seven minutes while you note on the form the strategies the student uses as well as his or her reading strengths and difficulties.

Students can monitor their own progress using the Student Checklist for Self-Assessment on page 10. Photocopy and laminate this form for each student. Review the checklist components with students many times, until they understand the purpose of the checklist and the meaning of each statement. Encourage students to mentally complete the checklist from time to time to track their own reading fluency.

To carry out what is called timed repeated reading, select a passage of text (150–200 words) that is at the student's independent reading level and that he or she has never read before. Have the student read aloud the passage for one minute. Track your own copy of the text while he or she reads, marking words omitted or pronounced incorrectly. Count the number of words the student read correctly. Then give the student three one-minute opportunities (in separate sessions) to read the same text, and average the scores to obtain his or her oral reading fluency rate.*

IN CONCLUSION

Does fluency instruction work? Research has shown that concentrated reading instruction can dramatically improve reading comprehension and fluency, which in turn affect academic performance, self-esteem, and overall achievement. With this in mind, it is not only helpful to instruct with an eye toward fluency, it is essential.

---

* For more detailed information on timed reading, consult Blevins (2001, pp. 9–12) and Rasinski (2003, pp. 82–83).

Teacher Rubric for Oral Reading Fluency

Child's Name: _____ Date: _____

Grade: _____ Passage: _____

For each category, circle the number that best describes the student's performance.

Accuracy

4	Recognizes most words; works to pronounce unfamiliar words, repeating them to self-correct if necessary.
3	Recognizes most words; works to pronounce unfamiliar words, self-correcting if necessary; sometimes requires assistance.
2	Struggles to decode and decipher words; hesitates before attempting to pronounce new words; usually requires assistance.
1	Recognizes very few words; makes no attempt to pronounce unfamiliar words.

Expression and Volume

4	Uses expression and volume that is natural to conversational language and that varies according to the content of the text.
3	Uses expression and volume that is appropriate to conversational language and the content of the text; sometimes hesitates when unsure of text.
2	Often speaks softly and in a monotone; pays little attention to expression or volume; focuses on getting through the text.
1	Reads words in a monotone and in a quiet voice.

Phrasing

4	Groups words into meaningful phrases or chunks of text.
3	Usually groups words into meaningful phrases or chunks of text.
2	Reads primarily in groups of two or three words.
1	Reads word by word without meaning.

Pace

4	Reads at a suitable pace and responds to punctuation with appropriate pausing and intonation.
3	Usually reads at a suitable pace and attends to most punctuation with appropriate pausing and intonation; halts at times when unsure.
2	Reads slowly, sometimes two or three words at a time; halts often; pays little attention to punctuation or pacing.
1	Reads words slowly in a string; does not heed punctuation.

Prosody

4	Attends to the rhythm of language, reading comfortably and without hesitating or halting.
3	Occasionally halts or runs sentences together when challenged by words or sentence structure.
2	Reads smoothly at times but most often slowly.
1	Reading sounds stilted and unnatural and lacks meaning.

Source: Adapted from "Training Teachers to Attend to Their Students' Oral Reading Fluency," by J. Zutell and T. V. Rasinski, 1991, *Theory Into Practice, 30,* pp. 211–217. Used with permission of the authors.

Fluency Practice Read-Aloud Plays: Grades 5–6   Scholastic Teaching Resources

Name: _____

How Carefully Do I Read?

	Most of the Time	Sometimes	Hardly Ever
1 I reread all or part of a sentence if it doesn't make sense.	☐	☐	☐
2 I try to pronounce every word, even words I have never seen before.	☐	☐	☐
3 I read a word again if it does not sound right.	☐	☐	☐
4 I use punctuation to guide the way I read, pausing or changing my tone of voice based on the punctuation.	☐	☐	☐
5 I try to read smoothly, without stopping after every word.	☐	☐	☐
6 I read with expression and speak clearly so others can hear me.	☐	☐	☐
7 I pay attention and am ready to speak when it is my turn.	☐	☐	☐

What I Need to Work on:

_____

_____

_____

_____

Source: Adapted from *35 Rubrics & Checklists to Assess Reading and Writing* by Adele Fiderer. Scholastic, 1998. Permission to reuse granted by the author.

Fluency Practice Read-Aloud Plays: Grades 5–6 Scholastic Teaching Resources

Using the Plays to Enhance Fluency

A Fluency Mini-Lesson

Let this sample mini-lesson serve as a model for using the plays to strengthen and assess reading fluency. The mini-lesson may be conducted with small groups or with the class as a whole.

READ-ALOUD PLAY 10

Babe Didrikson Zaharias

PREPARATION: Give each student a copy of the play "Babe Didrikson Zaharias" (pages 56–60). Note: For this model lesson, give students a copy of the same play. As they become more fluent, select different plays for each group to rehearse and perform.

Prereading

1. Introduce unfamiliar or difficult words students will come across in the text, such as *semi-professional, exceptional,* and *championship.* Help students decode the words. Review them several times to aid recognition and comprehension and boost fluency. (See Preparing for Difficult or Unfamiliar Text, page 13, for more.)

2. Review reading techniques that promote fluency, such as reading from left to right, "smooshing" words together, and crossing the page with a steady, sweeping eye movement (Blevins, 2001).

3. Divide the class into small groups, equal in size to the number of characters in the play.

Reading and Modeling

1. Model fluent reading before asking students to perform. As you read, point out ways in which your pacing, intonation, and expression lend meaning to the text. You might ask:

> "Did you notice how my voice rose at the end of the sentence 'This is amazing! Young Babe Didrikson has won five events and tied for first place in a sixth!'? An exclamation point lets us know the sentence tells something exciting; we use our voices to make it sound that way."

2. Try reading the sentences without the inflection. Observe aloud that questions read without the appropriate tone sound flat and stilted, without depth, character, or expression.

3. Then point out other punctuation marks that require voice or tone changes, for example, on page 59, the question mark in *Has Olympic competition been a lifelong goal for you?* and the period in *My goal was to be the greatest athlete that ever lived.*

4. Draw attention to the ways in which the play's meaning and a character's identity dictate the tone and volume of a character's speech. Help students differentiate between the conversational tone used by the man and woman from Employer's Casualty Company, who seek to hire Babe; the sensational, broadcasting tone used by the newscaster, who seeks to attract and hold an audience; and the playful tone used by Matt at the start of the play as he imitates a sports announcer.

5. Emphasize aspects of phonics and vocabulary that will increase students' understanding of language, encourage appropriately paced, accurate reading, and deepen comprehension. "Babe Didrikson Zaharias" presents opportunities to explore such topics as:

✳ **phrasing:** Readers must pause briefly after all commas. They will pause for a longer time after a comma that joins two sentences (*I love to compete, and I know I can win*) than after a comma that is preceded by a transitional word or phrase, such as *On the day of the qualifying championships, Babe competes in eight track events.*

✳ **use of an em-dash:** Be sure readers know how to respond to an em-dash, the long line that replaces an ellipsis and calls for a pause, as in *The second-place team scored 22 points, which is eight less than Didrikson scored—and they had 22 team members participating!*

✳ **multisyllabic words:** Provide students with tools for decoding words with four or more syllables, such as *competition*, *participate*, and *association*. Because many words contain syllables with similar spelling patterns, students can benefit from working with such patterns before tackling a new text. Help them practice breaking down words with similar prefix and suffix patterns to those found in the play. (In this play, such letter patterns would include *-dis* and *-tion*, among others.) With practice, students will learn to see these syllable chunks and readily recognize them as they read and decode. (Heilman, 2002)

Play Readability Scores

The chart below shows the readability scores of the plays in this collection. The texts were leveled using the Lexile Framework for Reading. These scores offer guidelines to help you select the plays that best match the needs and reading levels of each student. For more information about the Lexile Framework, go to www.lexile.com. (See Preparing for Difficult or Unfamiliar Text, below, for more.)

	Play Title	Lexile Score*
1.	The Crane Wife	600L
2.	The Women's Factory Strike	610L
3.	You're On!	620L
4.	Red Riding Hood—All Grown Up	630L
5.	Roller Coaster	660L
6.	The Pied Piper	680L
7.	Gold!	700L
8.	Volcano's Edge	710L
9.	The Four Dragons	720L
10.	Babe Didrikson Zaharias	740L
11.	On Top of the World	760L
12.	Strike from the Sky	800L
13.	The Plight of Persephone	860L
14.	Midnight Rescue	900L

* The Lexile score is based on dialogue text only. Conventional play formatting (such as the names that indicate which character is speaking) was removed during the scoring process.

A Lexile Score of **600 to 800** is appropriate for the fifth-grade independent reading level.

A Lexile Score of **700 to 900** is appropriate for the sixth-grade independent reading level.

Preparing for Difficult or Unfamiliar Text

To assess fluency, have students read text that is new to them (Blevins, 2001). With this in mind, when using the plays for assessment, do not prepare students by introducing unfamiliar or difficult words. Prereading may distort the assessment results.

Before reading for the purpose of *developing* fluency, however, it is helpful to highlight words that may prove to be stumbling blocks for struggling readers. Words slightly above grade level, difficult words on grade level, and complex high-frequency words can be daunting when encountered for the first time within text. To prevent this, introduce words and help students decode them before they read. Give them a chance to decipher the words before you provide correct pronunciation. Then review the words several times to aid recognition and boost fluency.

Using Readers Theater

Readers Theater offers a fun, interactive way to build fluency. Performing can be exciting, and the drive to present well can be a powerful force behind mastering fluency in reading and speech, motivating both struggling and proficient readers. By reading, rehearsing, and performing scripts at their independent reading levels, readers learn to navigate and use the written word in exciting, amusing, and purposeful ways. Readers Theater motivates students to experiment with language, working with expression, pacing, tone, inflection, meaning, and interpretation. To enhance the experience of Readers Theater consider these tips:

Limit Props

Props can distract readers and hinder the success of fluent reading. If you do include them, make them simple and easy to hold. Since scripts are meant to be read aloud rather than memorized, it is important that every reader has one hand free to hold the script.

Treat Scripts as Stories

With the purpose of building strong readers ever in sight, treat the text of a play in much the same way as the text of a story. Read the title with students. Anticipate what the play might be about, and predict outcomes, conflicts, and character behaviors. Invite students to tell how they feel about the plot of the play. See A Fluency Mini-Lesson, page 11, for more ideas on using the plays to boost reading skills.

Heed Clues for Direction

Help students recognize hints in both stage directions and dialogue text that indicate physical movement as well as the pitch, emotion, or volume of speech. For example, words spelled in all capital letters are generally intended to be shouted. Stage directions often indicate not only activity (*stepping forward*) but appropriate tone of voice (for example, *alarmed*). It's helpful to give audience members copies of the plays so that they can read along.

Develop Prosody

Prosody, or the rhythm of language, comes alive in Readers Theater—but only when readers are able to read their text easily. Students need to read and reread their scripts many times in order to feel comfortable reading their own character's lines and understanding the purpose and flow of the play. Encourage readers to work first in pairs, and then in small groups and individually, to practice the text until they feel comfortable reading it aloud.

Consider Placement

When performing Readers Theater, it's effective for students to stand so they can be seen and heard. Have readers face the person(s) to whom they are speaking, and have the narrator speak directly to the audience. It works well to have all performers "onstage" at once, standing in a semi-circle and facing the audience. As your students grow with Readers Theater, movement and staging can be added to the performance, if desired.

Encourage Teamwork

Encourage readers to pay attention not only to their own lines but to those of fellow performers. Reading along while others speak their lines will promote fluent reading and will ensure that each performer is ready when his or her turn comes along.

Resources for Reading Fluency, Comprehension, and Readers Theater

Armbruster, Bonnie B., Fran Lehr, and Jean Osborn. *Put Reading First: The Research Building Blocks for Teaching Children to Read.* (Center for the Improvement of Early Reading Achievement and the National Institute for Literacy. Office of Educational Research and Improvement, U.S. Department of Education, 2001).

Blevins, Wiley. *Building Fluency: Lessons and Strategies for Reading Success.* New York: Scholastic, 2001.*

Charlton, Beth Critchley. *Informal Assessment Strategies.* Ontario, Canada: Pembroke Publishers, 2005.

Clay, Marie M. *Becoming Literate: The Construction of Inner Control.* Portsmouth, NH: Heinemann, 1991.

Cunningham, Patricia M. and Richard L. Allington. *Classrooms That Work: They Can ALL Read and Write.* New York: Pearson Education, 2003.

Fiderer, Adele. *35 Rubrics & Checklists to Assess Reading and Writing.* New York: Scholastic, 1998.

Fountas, Irene C. and Gay Su Pinnell. *Guiding Readers and Writers.* Portsmouth, NH: Heinemann, 2001.

Heilman, Arthur W. *Phonics in Perspective.* Upper Saddle River, NJ: Pearson Education, 2002.

Lyon, G. Reid. "Why Reading Is Not a Natural Process." *Educational Leadership*, Volume 55, No. 6 (March 1998): pp. 14–18.

Lyon, G. Reid and Vinita Chhabra. "The Science of Reading Research." *Educational Leadership*, Volume 61, No. 6 (March 2004): pp. 12–17.

Pinnell, Gay Su and Patricia L. Scharer. *Teaching for Comprehension in Reading.* New York: Scholastic, 2003.*

Rasinski, Timothy V. "Creating Fluent Readers," *Educational Leadership*, Volume 61, No. 6 (March 2004): pp. 46–51.

Rasinski, Timothy V. *The Fluent Reader.* New York: Scholastic, 2003.

Rasinski, Timothy V. *3-Minute Reading Assessments: Word Recognition, Fluency, and Comprehension, Grades 1–4.* New York: Scholastic, 2005.

Torgesen, J. K. "The Prevention of Reading Difficulties." *Journal of School Psychology*, Volume 40, Issue 1, pp. 7–26.

Worthy, Jo and Karen Broaddus. "Fluency Beyond the Primary Grades: From Group Performance to Silent, Independent Reading." *The Reading Teacher*, Volume 55, No. 4, pp. 334–343.

Worthy, Jo and Kathryn Prater. "I Thought About It All Night: Readers Theatre for Reading Fluency and Motivation (The Intermediate Grades)." *The Reading Teacher*, Volume 56, No. 3 (November 2002): p. 294.

Worthy, Jo. *Readers Theater for Building Fluency.* New York: Scholastic, 2005.

Yopp, Hallie Kay and Ruth Helen Yopp. "Supporting Phonemic Awareness Development in the Classroom." *The Reading Teacher*, Volume 54, No. 2 (October 2000): pp. 130–143.

* This resource includes samples and/or examples of phrase-cued text.

The Crane Wife

✳ Adapted from a Japanese Tale ✳

CHARACTERS

Narrator 1	Narrator 2	Woman	Crane
Old Man	Fisherman	Emperor	

Narrator 1:   There once lived an old man who earned his living making charcoal for people to burn in their stoves. He worked hard, but he earned little money and was poor.

Old Man: I have labored my entire life and saved what little I could all these years. Finally, I have enough money to buy a sleeping mattress. No longer will I sleep on the bare floor!

Narrator 2:   The next day, the man set out for the market. He walked down the long, dusty road toward town.

(*He comes upon a fisherman who has trapped a crane in his fishing net.*)

Fisherman: Ha! Ha! Ha! Look at that gawky crane, struggling to free herself from my sturdy net! She'll never break loose! Ha! Ha! Ha!

Fluency Practice Read-Aloud Plays: Grades 5–6 • Scholastic Teaching Resources

Old Man:	Young man! Let that bird free!
Fisherman:	(*laughing*) It's just a bird. What do you care?
Old Man:	That bird has done nothing to you. (*He reaches into his pocket.*) Look; here is the money I have saved to buy myself a mattress. I will give you this money in exchange for the crane's freedom. Take my money, and release her.

(*The fisherman takes the money and sets the crane free. The crane immediately soars to the sky and flies away.*)

Old Man:	(*to himself as he walks back home*) All my savings are gone. I have worked hard, and yet I have nothing to show for it. (*He smiles.*) The crane is free, though! What a beautiful, glorious bird!
Narrator 1:	That night, the old man heard a knock at his door. When he opened the door, there stood a stunning young woman.
Old Man:	May I help you?
Woman:	I wish to be your wife.
Old Man:	I am old and poor. Why would you want to marry me?
Woman:	I have seen that you are kind and gentle. I know you have worked hard, and it's time someone cared for you. I want to do that.
Old Man:	I would be honored to call you my wife.
Narrator 2:	For years, the old man and his wife lived in happiness together. She became a loving wife and cared for him. He wished only that he had more money so he could buy her beautiful clothes and provide a more comfortable home.

Old Man: (*sitting by the fireplace*) I wish I had more money to provide for you.

Woman: Perhaps I can help you, my dear husband. I must to go into that little room and close the door. I will be in there for hours, and you must promise me not to open the door.

Old Man: Whatever you wish, I will do.

Narrator 1: Hours passed, and his wife finally came out of the room. In her arms she carried the finest white fabric ever made.

Woman: Take this fine cloth to the Emperor. He will pay you handsomely for it.

Narrator 2: The old man met with the emperor the next day.

Emperor: (*He admires the cloth.*) This is the most beautiful cloth I've ever seen! Here, take this money in exchange. (*He pays the old man.*)

Narrator 1: Several years pass.

Old Man: (*sitting by the fire again*) With the money we got for the cloth, we built a fine home, enjoyed plenty of food and bought nice clothes. But now the money has run out, and I have no way to replace it.

Woman: Once again, I will go into that little room and close the door. I will be in there for several hours, but remember . . . you must promise me not to open the door.

Narrator 2: Again, hours passed and the wife came out with fine cloth. Again, the old man took it to the Emperor and came home with a sack full of coins. The man and his wife lived on this money for quite some time. Eventually, the money again ran out, and the man felt despair.

Fluency Practice Read-Aloud Plays: Grades 5–6 • Scholastic Teaching Resources

Woman: If it will please you, I will make some more cloth.

(She goes into the little room and closes the door.)

Old Man: I am curious to know how my wife makes that beautiful cloth. What can she possibly use to spin such exquisite fabric? Surely one little peek will not hurt.

Narrator 1: The old man cracked open the door, and to his surprise, there stood the beautiful white crane he had saved so long ago.

Crane: *(sadly)* Yes, it is I, the crane you once saved. I became your wife that night to thank you for saving my life. Now that you have discovered my secret, I can no longer stay here.

(She flies out an open window. The man rushes outside, calling after her.)

Old Man: How could I have been so foolish? Because of my curiosity, I have lost the only love I have known!

Narrator 2: Days later, the man walked to the sea and watched cranes nesting on an island on the water. He saw one who looked taller and more beautiful than the rest. Sighing, the old man shook his head.

Old Man: That is my crane wife, as beautiful outside as she is within. Truly, this creature is Queen of the Cranes.

THE END

Fluency Practice Read-Aloud Plays: Grades 5–6 • Scholastic Teaching Resources

The Women's Factory Strike

Fluency Practice Read-Aloud Plays: Grades 5–6   Scholastic Teaching Resources

CHARACTERS

Narrator 1

Narrator 2

Henry, a factory manager

Neil, a factory owner

Natalie

Margaret

Renee

Maria

Karen

Man

Narrator 1:	It is November 1909. Five hundred women and girls operate sewing machines in a shirt factory in New York City.
Narrator 2:	Above the hum of machines, the women hear loud voices coming from an office inside the factory.
Henry:	(*loudly*) I don't like the way this company treats workers! You yell at those girls all day long. You make them work from morning till night without stopping! They can't even take a lunch break!
Neil:	That's the way I run things around here, Henry. If you don't like it, go work somewhere else.
Henry:	You'd better believe I will. I won't treat my workers like you do. I'm taking them to a company where bosses know how to treat their workers!

Neil:	You're not taking those girls anywhere, Henry. You're fired! (*to his assistants*) Get him out of here! NOW!
Narrator 1:	Sewing machines stop on the factory floor as the women and girls listen to the shouting. The office door slams open, and two burly men drag Henry out of the small room and across the factory floor toward the exit.
Henry:	If Neil wants me out, let him take me himself!
Neil:	This is my factory! You—and everyone else in here—will do as I say. (*to the men*) Throw him outside. (*Neil points to the women and girls.*) GET BACK TO WORK!
Henry:	(*yelling as he's dragged away*) Girls! Will you stay at your machines and see a fellow worker treated this way?
Narrator 2:	The men tossed Henry out the door, into the snow.
Natalie:	(*taking a deep breath and standing up*) I won't stand by and watch a kind man be mistreated. I quit! (*She picks up her coat and walks out the factory door.*)
Narrator 1:	As soon as Natalie left, other women stood up.
Margaret:	(*shouting to the workers*) I'm with Natalie. Henry is a good man. I protest his being treated that way!
Renee:	(*also shouting*) And I protest our being so badly treated!
Maria:	Why should we work such long hours for such little pay?
Margaret:	We work fourteen hours a day, every day. And what do we get? TWO DOLLARS A WEEK! It's absurd!
Karen:	We aren't allowed breaks or even to go to the bathroom without Neil taking money from our pay!

Renee: Sometimes we have to take sewing home at night!

Margaret, Renee, Maria, and Karen: We've had it! We quit!

Neil: (*in a furious, booming voice*) Get back to your machines! If you leave this job, I'll see to it that you never come back—not to this factory or any other!

Narrator 2: Neil's voice was drowned out as hundreds of women and girls walked toward the factory entrance.

Narrator 1: Four hundred women streamed out the door and into the November snow.

Neil: Let them go, boys. Their "strike" won't last more than a day, for women just aren't strong enough to keep it up. They'll come crawling back, just you wait.

Narrator 2: That night, some workers gathered at Natalie's house.

Renee: So then, we're all in this together? We're going on strike?

Margaret: Women at other factories are on strike, too. They refuse to go to work until employers agree to treat them well.

Maria: We deserve to be treated with respect.

Karen: And we deserve fair pay for our work.

Natalie: I'll be on that picket line tomorrow. Just give me a sign to carry.

Narrator 1: The next morning, Natalie, Margaret, Renee, Maria, and Karen joined hundreds of other women walking up and down the icy sidewalk in front of their factory.

Fluency Practice Read-Aloud Plays: Grades 5–6 • Scholastic Teaching Resources

Karen:	(*stopping a man walking by*) Please show your support! Insist that women be treated fairly in the workplace!
Narrator 2:	The man shoves Karen, knocking her to the ground.
Man:	I'll rough up anyone who tells me that garbage again.
Narrator 1:	Across the city, many men yelled at, pushed, and frightened those on the picket line. Still, girls and women continued to march, telling everyone who passed by about the poor treatment they had received in the factory.
Narrator 2:	The strike lasted more than 100 days and involved factories all over the city. By the end, more than 30,000 women had left their factory seats, joined the picket line, and demanded fair working conditions. Many husbands, brothers, and other men joined to show their support.
Narrator 1:	Finally, their efforts paid off. Factory owners needed their employees back and agreed to make changes.
Natalie:	(*to the others one afternoon*) Did you hear the news? We did it! We're getting better pay, shorter hours, breaks during the workday, vacation time, and more!
Margaret:	We got what we need and deserve!
Maria:	This strike belonged to young girls, married women, American citizens and immigrants. It belonged to those who speak English and those who don't.
Natalie:	On the picket line, it didn't matter what language we spoke. We all wanted the same thing. Now it's ours!

❈ THE END ❈

You're On!

Max: (*facing the audience*) Welcome to You're On!, the brightest game show on earth! I'm your host, Max Power, and our topic today is renewable energy sources! Let's meet today's contestants, shall we?

(*Max points toward the contestants, who are standing behind their microphones.*)

Max: Please welcome contestants Gail Force, Gus Ting, and Summer Breeze! (*Gail, Gus and Summer wave to the audience.*) Contestants, are you ready to play today's game?

(*The contestants nod.*)

Max: All right, then…You're On!

(*Music plays, and the contestants look at a TV screen.*)

Max: Today's first question, for 200 dollars, is: WHAT IS RENEWABLE ENERGY?

Fluency Practice Read-Aloud Plays: Grades 5–6 • Scholastic Teaching Resources

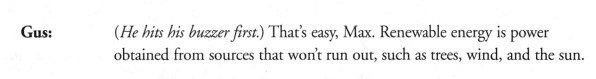

Gus:	(*He hits his buzzer first.*) That's easy, Max. Renewable energy is power obtained from sources that won't run out, such as trees, wind, and the sun.
Max:	Excellent answer! You've earned 200 dollars, Gus. Now let's move on to our next question: WHAT IS SOLAR ENERGY?
Gus:	(*He hits his buzzer first again.*) Solar energy is the heat produced from the light of the sun. People take advantage of solar energy by spending time outside during the day, when the sun is shining. Some people put solar panels on their roofs and harness the sun's energy that way.
Gail:	I object! The contestant gave more information than he was asked to give!
Max:	This is not a courtroom, Gail. You really can't object.
Gail:	He'd better not get additional points for the information he tacked on.
Max:	His answer was correct, so he gets the amount offered, which was 200 dollars. Next question: HOW DO PEOPLE HARNESS THE SUN'S ENERGY?
Gus:	(*He hits his buzzer first again.*) Some people put solar panels on their roofs. Heat from the sun collects in the panels and stays there. After the sun goes down, the panels provide power from the heat they've stored.
Gail:	Are you going to let him have that? He already answered that question!
Summer:	I have to agree, Max. It does seem as though you gave him an easy one.
Max:	I asked all of you the question. Any one of you were eligible to answer it.
Gail:	(*to Summer*) He's got to be cheating. Maybe his buzzer's the only one that works. Try yours.

(*Summer hits her buzzer, and it lights up.*)

Max: Oh, Summer! Too bad you hit your buzzer before I asked the question! Buzzing before the question results in an automatic free turn for the player on your left. That would be Gus.

(*Gail groans loudly while Summer shakes her head in disbelief.*)

Max: Gus, for 1,000 bonus bucks, can you tell me three kinds of renewable energy and their sources?

Gus: Yes, I can, Max. One is solar energy, which comes from the sun. A second is wind energy, which comes from wind, or moving air. A third is hydro-electric energy, which comes from fast-flowing water, such as a waterfall.

Gail: (*waving her hand in the air*) I'm ready for the next question, Max.

Max: Excellent. Ready, you three? For six hundred dollars, tell me: HOW DO WE HARNESS WIND ENERGY AND WHAT DO WE USE IT FOR?

Gail: (*She hits her buzzer first.*) Wind energy comes from moving air. Air pushes on the blades of large windmills or generators, and when they turn, this creates power. People use air power to provide electricity to operate lights, TV's, toasters, and anything that plugs in.

Max: Outstanding! You've earned 600 dollars! The current score is Gus, 1400 dollars, Gail, 600 dollars, and Summer, nothing. Now get ready for the final question, worth 1600 dollars! Whoever gets it will be today's winner!

(*The contestants lean forward, each ready to press a buzzer.*)

Max: WHY IS IT IMPORTANT FOR HOSPITALS, SUPERMARKETS, AND OTHER PUBLIC PLACES TO HAVE BACK-UP GENERATORS ON HAND TO PROVIDE POWER?

Fluency Practice Read-Aloud Plays: Grades 5–6 • Scholastic Teaching Resources

(Right then, the power shuts down in the studio and all goes black.)

Summer: My buzzer doesn't work! It doesn't work, and I know I hit it first!

**Gail and
Gus:** No, I did! I did!

Max: *(He calls out the answer because his microphone has no power.)* I guess we're seeing the reason firsthand, folks! Most places use generators to provide power when the electricity goes out due to lightning or some kind of power failure! That helps prevent problems like the one we're having right now!

Summer: *(speaking from out of the darkness)* Does this TV studio have a generator, Max? Will the power come on so we can finish the game?

Max: I'm sorry, Summer, but generators cost money, and our studio hasn't been able to afford one yet. So, that's the end of today's show! *(He speaks to the audience.)* Today's game could not be completed, so the players are disqualified. But look on the bright side: no one can win, so no one can go home a loser! Thank you for watching today, and be sure to tune in tomorrow to America's premier energy game show... You're On!

 THE END

Red Riding Hood— All Grown Up

CHARACTERS

Narrator
Red Riding Hood
Walter Woodcutter
Grandma
Ticket Seller
Woman
Wolf

SCENE ONE

Narrator: Once upon a time, in a lush, fragrant forest, there lived a woman named Red Riding Hood. She lived in a costly mansion, bought with the wealth she had earned in her younger days by accidentally starring as the main character in the beloved tale Little Red Riding Hood.

(*Red sits cross-legged on a hammock and paints her long fingernails.*)

Red: (*crossly*) Walter! Come here!

Walter: (*rushing toward Red*) What is it, Darling?

Red: (*in a bossy tone*) Hold this hammock still for me. It sways while I try to paint my fingernails with this ravishing red polish.

Walter: (*sincerely*) I would like to, Honey, but I'm on my way to work, and holding this hammock will make me late.

Fluency Practice Read-Aloud Plays: Grades 5–6 · Scholastic Teaching Resources

Red: *(still cross)* You cut down trees in the woods by yourself! Who would know if you were late? I'd rather you did something important with your day, like keep me company. *(threatening)* Aren't I important to you?

Walter: *(sighing)* Of course, Red, but my job is important, too. We've been over this a hundred times. I'm not just a woodcutter, I'm the Official Forest Safety Officer! If I didn't go to work, who would protect people from wolves in the woods? What if I hadn't been working ten years ago when you needed help?

Red: That's old news, Walter. You saved my life, and I said thank you. I even fell in love with you and married you when I grew up. Can't we move on?

Walter: *(leaving)* Try to enjoy your day, Sweetheart, and I promise I'll be home by sunset.

(Red scowls, puts down the polish, and waves her nails to dry them.)

Red: *(imitating Walter's deep voice)* Try to enjoy yourself. How on earth will I ever do that? There is nothing to do around here! My life is so boring!

(Red's elderly grandmother hobbles around the backyard gate.)

Grandma: Good morning, Red. I brought you a basket of muffins, just like I have every day since you and Walter saved me from that beastly wolf ten years ago!

(Red grabs the basket and rudely shuffles through the cloth inside, pulling out a plump blueberry muffin and taking a bite.)

Red: *(groaning and talking with her mouth full)* Ten years ago! That's all you and Walter talk about! You've been bringing me the same muffins and remembering the same event for TEN YEARS! Does this make SENSE to you, Grandma?

Grandma: (*shocked and a little offended*) My goodness, Red, you sound a bit uppity today. (*She softens.*) Maybe you're catching a cold. Why aren't you wearing that warm red cape I made you?

Red: If you want to know the truth, I don't wear it anymore. I've had it with red capes, muffins, and woodcutters saving the day. I want to go someplace else, Grandma! I want to make a difference!

Grandma: That's certainly a valiant dream, Honey. We all want to make a difference in this world. (*She reaches for Red's hand.*) How pretty your nails look. Want me to help you paint your toes?

Red: (*considering*) Sure, why not?

SCENE TWO

Narrator: Red continued to feel frustrated about her life and how stifled she felt. That afternoon, after Grandma went back to her bungalow, Red packed a bag and set off.

(*Red walks along, carrying a heavy suitcase.*)

Red: Boy, it's hot out here, and this bag is heavy. I'm at the edge of the woods, though, and not far from the bus station. Soon I'll be on my way to a whole new world!

(*Red approaches the ticket booth at the bus station.*)

Ticket Seller: Where to, Miss?

Red: I don't know, really. I hadn't given it much thought. I want to go someplace free and relaxing.

Ticket Seller: Bus tickets aren't free. Now where would you like to go?

Fluency Practice Read-Aloud Plays: Grades 5–6 Scholastic Teaching Resources

Red: Well, I've heard Palm Springs is nice, and the Florida Keys sure are warm. Oh, and I've seen pictures of the Grand Canyon, too. THAT looks pretty impressive, don't you think?

Ticket Seller: There are people behind you. Can you just decide?

Red: (*thinking*) Then again, I want to make a difference. Where can I go where I'll be able to make a difference?

(*The woman next in line taps Red on the shoulder.*)

Woman: You'll be making a BIG difference if you get out of line and let the rest of us buy tickets. We've got buses to catch.

(*Startled, Red steps out of line and wanders over to a stand of brochures. As she reads one, a wolf approaches, disguised in a trench coat and hat.*)

Wolf: Excuse me, but I couldn't help hearing you say that you're looking to make a difference. Why, I have just the opportunity. You see, I run a preschool down the road, and one of the students ate the head teacher—I mean the head teacher got a job elsewhere—and now those poor students have no teacher, at such a tender time in their young lives! They stand at the threshold of learning and with no one to teach them the way!

Red: (*overjoyed*) Why, that sounds just like a job I would enjoy! I can teach young children, and I'd love to make a difference in their day!

(*Smiling slyly, the wolf leads Red out of the bus station and down the road. Seconds later, Walter runs into the station.*)

Walter: (*to the ticket seller*) Have you seen my wife? She's five feet, four inches, and . . . well, I don't know what she's wearing today, but she used to wear a long, red cape!

Ticket Seller: Was that Red Riding Hood, all grown up? I thought she looked familiar! A celebrity, right here in my station! She went out the door a few minutes ago with a man in a trench coat. He was fixing to make her a teacher at his preschool... said the students ate the last teacher.

Walter: A trench coat and hat? That's no man she's with—it's a wolf! It must be the nephew of the wolf I saved Red from. He dressed in people's clothes, too! I just knew that nephew had been lurking around, waiting for his chance! Which way did they go?

(*The Ticket Seller points to the door, and Walter rushes out.*)

SCENE THREE

Narrator: As soon as Red and the wolf walk a safe distance from the bus station, the wolf stops.

Wolf: (*putting down Red's suitcase*) This thing weighs a ton. What do you have in here anyway?

Red: This and that. (*looking around*) I don't see a school here. Is it much farther?

Wolf: (*baring his teeth*) No, I think we're just about there!

(*The wolf leaps up and grabs Red's hand, squeezing it tightly.*)

Red: (*screaming*) Hey! Let go of me! Let go, I say!

Wolf: Didn't I say the students ate the teacher? Well, I'm the only student in this school, and I'm hungry!

Walter: (*He runs into view, panting and holding his side.*) Darn runner's cramps! They get me every time. I've got to learn to breathe right when I run.

Fluency Practice Read-Aloud Plays: Grades 5–6 • Scholastic Teaching Resources

Wolf: (*irritated*) Oh, here he comes to save the day. Beat it, woodcutter! I've got her, and there's nothing you can do to stop me. (*He starts to drag Red into the forest.*) I'm going to devour every part of her, from her ten tasty toes to her bright red fingernails.

(*Suddenly, the wolf looks at Red's hands and gasps.*)

Wolf: Oh, no! Is that nail polish you're wearing?

Red: Yes; do you like it?

Wolf: I'm allergic to nail polish! If it even touches my tongue, I break out in a nasty rash and my throat closes up and I can't breathe! Is it on your toes, too?

Red: Yes! And I spilled some on my fingers. I'm not sure exactly which ones... (*She studies her hands.*)

(*The wolf lets Red go and runs off. Red stands and looks at Walter.*)

Walter: (*picking up Red's suitcase*) Red, I've been thinking. Maybe you should have a job, you know, in our forest.

Red: (*walking beside him, excited*) I could teach school to the animals of the forest! Why, those animals are just waiting for an education! I could really make a difference... and Grandma, she could teach baking....

(*They walk off.*)

❊ THE END ❊

Fluency Practice Read-Aloud Plays: Grades 5–6   Scholastic Teaching Resources

Roller Coaster!

CHARACTERS

Narrator	Diego
Ms. Peach	Alex
Mr. Toole	Marla
Mr. Wade	

Fluency Practice Read-Aloud Plays: Grades 5–6   Scholastic Teaching Resources

Narrator: One Monday morning, Ms. Peach's fourth graders went on a field trip to Cascade Amusement Park.

(*Students gather at the entrance to the park.*)

Ms. Peach: (*speaking loudly so everyone can hear*) We are about to go into the park. Remember, this is a science field trip. We're here to learn how roller coasters work!

(*A man steps forward to speak to the group.*)

Mr. Toole: Good morning, kids. My name is Mr. Toole, and I'll be your tour guide today. I know everything there is to know about roller coasters and how they work.

(*A man steps up beside Mr. Toole and gives him a suspicious look.*)

Mr. Toole: (*pleasantly*) May I help you, sir?

Mr. Wade: I should be asking you that question. I'm the tour guide here, but who are you?

Mr. Toole: (*He shakes his head and laughs nervously.*) Why, I've never seen you before. I'm sure you don't work for this park.

Mr. Wade: (*angry*) Of course I do!

Ms. Peach: (*stepping forward*) I don't know which of you is the real tour guide, but we need to get started. (*She glances at her watch.*) Our bus leaves in three hours.

Mr. Toole: (*addressing the group*) Of course. Now, as I was saying, I know everything there is to know about roller coasters. The first roller coaster on wheels was invented in Russia in 1784. People in Paris made one shortly after that. They called it a roller coaster because the track was made of rolling parts and the cars were actually sleds, or coasters. The coasters would slide down the track, slipping down over the rollers.

Diego: Wow, that sounds dangerous. Did people get hurt?

Mr. Toole: You bet they did. Many times, the cars just kept on going and ran right off the track!

Alex: Why did people go on them if they could get hurt?

Mr. Toole: The thrill of the ride, of course! Anyway, the first rides happened in two parts. First, the riders rolled down the hill to the bottom. Then they got out, and park workers had to carry the coaster all the way to the top of the hill so the next group of riders could slide down.

Marla: That's a ton of work!

Diego: I wouldn't want that job.

Mr. Toole: Exactly. That's why engineers have spent centuries making roller coasters safer and motorized!

Alex: By motorized, do you mean they have engines?

Mr. Toole:	Yes. The more powerful the engine, the faster the roller coaster.
Mr. Wade:	(*stepping forward*) I disagree.
Mr. Toole:	You can't disagree with me. I'm the tour guide.
Mr. Wade:	I'm the tour guide, and you're giving these students the wrong information. You may know the history of the first roller coasters, but you don't know the science of modern ones. (*He turns to face the students.*) Boys and girls, the motor on a roller coaster is only used to bring the cars to the top of the hill. After that, it is the physics of motion that causes the cars to speed down the track.
Alex:	(*alarmed*) So when we're zooming down the hill, there won't be an engine that keeps us from going too fast?
Mr. Wade:	How fast the coaster goes has nothing to do with an engine. It has to do with the height of the hill and the slope of the track.
Ms. Peach:	(*rubbing her forehead*) We don't understand.
Mr. Wade:	Think about two slides at a playground. One is very tall, and you have to climb fifty steps to get to the top. The other is much shorter. It takes only eight steps to get to the top. Which slide is going to give you a faster ride?
Diego:	The taller slide.
Mr. Wade:	Exactly! Why is that?
Marla:	Because you're up higher, so you come down a steeper slope?
Mr. Wade:	That's right. The taller slide is steeper and straighter. How does that affect your ride?
Alex:	Well, you slide almost straight down, and you go fast.

Fluency Practice Read-Aloud Plays: Grades 5–6   Scholastic Teaching Resources

Diego: I get it! That's why you slide so slowly on a short slide. The short slide isn't steep, so you almost have to push yourself to start sliding. And when you do go down, the slide isn't steep enough for gravity to pull you much. Sliding on a small slide is gentle and slow. Sometimes you completely stop moving before you even get to the bottom.

Mr. Wade: Now compare that to a roller coaster. The motor pulls the heavy coaster to the top of a steep hill. The cars pause for a moment at the top, and the motor shuts off. The coaster balances for a moment and then goes racing down.

Marla: It's pulled by its own weight!

Ms. Peach: And then does the motor turn on again, to pull the cars up the next hill?

Mr. Wade: That depends on the track. If the first hill is very steep, and the bottom of the hill is gently curved, the coaster will speed down the first hill. Then it will slow down on the slope but will still have enough speed to coast up the second hill.

Alex: When it gets to the top of the next hill, the same thing happens again, right? The weight of the coaster pulls it down a second hill?

Mr. Wade: Exactly! And again, a gentle slope at the bottom ensures that the cars will slow down instead of speeding off the track.

Diego: Are there brakes on a roller coaster, Mr. Wade?

Mr. Wade: Yes. Workers check the brakes and every part of the coasters every day to make sure each ride is safe.

Ms. Peach: We have learned a lot about roller coasters, thanks to both of you! You should work as a team! Now class, let's get in line for our first ride, which will be on the Cocoon!

(As Ms. Peach leads the class to the Cocoon, Mr. Toole and Mr. Wade shake hands.)

Mr. Toole: I must admit, I am a visiting tour guide.

Mr. Wade: You know so much about the history of coasters!

Mr. Toole: And you about roller coasters today! We should work together.

(*They walk off toward the main office. Ms. Peach and the students climb into the cars of the Cocoon. They sit down and lower safety bars to keep them in their seats. An engine starts to move the coaster up a steep hill.*)

Marla: I hear the engine working to pull us up!

(*The coaster stops at the top of the hill.*)

Diego: Now the engine has shut off. We're on our own!

Narrator: The class screams as the coaster races down the track. Then the coaster runs across a gentle slope and up the next hill.

Alex: (*yelling*) Good thing that was a gentle slope!

Narrator: The roller coaster climbs the second hill and rushes down the other side. Then it rolls onto a long, sloping track and comes to a halt.

Ms. Peach: Wow! That was a short ride, but a fast one!

Diego: I was really scared about riding roller coasters. Now that I know how they work, I can really enjoy myself!

Marla: Just check out the slope before you ride, Diego. As long as it's gradual, the car will slow down!

Ms. Peach: Mr. Toole and Mr. Wade might have to worry about their jobs! From what I'm hearing, we have new experts on board!

 THE END

Fluency Practice Read-Aloud Plays: Grades 5–6   Scholastic Teaching Resources

The Pied Piper

Adapted from Robert Browning's poem
"The Pied Piper of Hamelin"

CHARACTERS

Narrator	Jimmy
Maria	Julie
Phil	Crowd
Felix	The Pied Piper
Mayor	Amy

Narrator: Long ago, nestled at the edge of the River Weser in Germany, the small town of Hamelin suffered with an enormous problem.

Maria: Our town is infested with rats! Hundreds and hundreds of rats run through the streets, invading our homes, eating our cheese, and slurping our soups!

Phil: The varmints run through our fields, our churches, and our streets, eating everything in sight! Something must be done to stop them!

Felix: Where is that lazy mayor of ours? He should be doing something to rid Hamelin of this curse!

(*Maria, Amy, Phil, Felix, Jimmy, and Julie run to the Mayor's home. They knock on the door and wait.*)

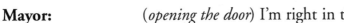

Mayor:	(*opening the door*) I'm right in the middle of my nap, so come back later.
Jimmy:	With all due respect, sir, we don't have time to come back later! Haven't you seen the rats in our streets? Why, we can barely walk without stepping on them!
Mayor:	Then step on them and be rid of them.

(*He starts to close the door, but Julie holds it open.*)

Julie:	The rats are too numerous, Mayor, and they are enormous! Even our cats and dogs are afraid of them, so fierce and so numerous are these rats! We must stop the rodents from taking over our town. What are you going to do?
Mayor:	I'll think about it in my sleep. (*He shuts the door.*)
Narrator:	An angry crowd gathered outside the mayor's home.
Crowd:	(*chanting*) Stop the rats! Stop the rats!
Pied Piper:	(*stepping forward*) Excuse me, but I think I can help you solve this problem. Schedule a meeting for me with your mayor so that I can tell him my fee. If he agrees to pay what I ask, I will rid your town of rats today.

(*Amy and Jimmy pound on the mayor's front door.*)

Crowd:	Wake up and hear this man!
Mayor:	(*angrily*) How dare you interrupt my sleep! You will pay dearly for such an intrusion!
Julie:	(*pointing to the piper*) This man says he can rid our town of the rats . . . today! You must listen to him.

Fluency Practice Read-Aloud Plays: Grades 5–6 Scholastic Teaching Resources

Mayor:	(*looking down as six rats run between his legs and into his house*) Young man, I'm sure you are wasting my time. You are only one man, and a scrawny one at that. How do you intend to get rid of our rats in one day?
Pied Piper:	I have my ways, and to do the job, my fee is fifty thousand dollars.
Mayor:	(*gasping*) Fifty thousand dollars? That's an outrageous amount, and I will not pay it!
Pied Piper:	Keep your money, then—and your rats. (*He walks away.*)
Crowd:	(*shouting*) Hire him! Hire him! Don't let him leave!
Mayor:	(*rolling his eyes*) All right, we'll pay you what you ask, fifty thousand dollars to get rid of our rats. But we won't pay you a cent until every last rodent is gone.
Pied Piper:	(*shaking the mayor's hand*) It's a deal, then.
Narrator:	With that, the piper took a slim flute from his pocket, walked slowly through the crowd, and began to play. Within seconds, rats came running from every corner of Hamelin, falling in line behind the piper.
Crowd:	(*screaming*) Rats are coming from all over! But look how they follow him in rows; it's amazing! That piper is leading the rats out of our town!
Maria:	Look! He's heading for the cliff!
Jimmy:	He's standing on the edge of the cliff, and the rats are still following him!
Amy:	Now he's stepped aside, but the rats still march, plunging off the cliff and to their deaths below!

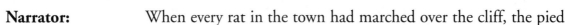

Narrator:	When every rat in the town had marched over the cliff, the pied piper came back to the mayor's house.
Pied Piper:	(*knocking at the door*) All right, sir, the rats are gone. Now pay me my fifty thousand, and I'll be on my way.
Mayor:	(*laughing*) Surely you can't be serious! I don't have money to give to strangers for playing a flute! Those rats ran away on their own. I owe you nothing. (*He hands the pied piper a fifty dollar bill.*) But here is fifty dollars for the melody you played.
Pied Piper:	(*to the townspeople*) Will you not stand up for me? Will you not see that the mayor pays me the sum he agreed to before I took the rats away?
Maria:	(*turning away*) The rats are gone.
Amy:	I don't think they were ever that bad to begin with.
Phil:	Go your way; fifty dollars is more than enough.
Pied Piper:	(*to the crowd*) I cannot believe this! I rescued you and yet you snub me! Well, watch your backs, people of Hamelin! You have cheated me so that it would not cost you fifty thousand, but your selfishness will cost you much, much more!

(*The pied piper storms out of town.*)

Felix:	(*laughing*) What loss is it to us? We got what we wanted. We are free of rats at last!
Julie:	(*worried*) I don't know, Felix. I think we might really regret this.
Narrator:	Darkness fell over Hamelin, and the moon did not shine that night. Out of the pitch black, the people heard the sound of a mournful flute.

Fluency Practice Read-Aloud Plays: Grades 5–6 • Scholastic Teaching Resources

Amy: Oh, it is probably that funny stranger, playing out his sorrows on the cliff.

Jimmy: The flute is growing louder and more fierce.

Mayor: (*opening the door to his house*) What is that racket, interrupting my nightly rest?

Narrator: At that moment, the pied piper appeared on the cliff, playing a dark tune on his flute and marching toward the town. The people gasped, horrified at what they saw behind him.

Maria: It's a herd of huge animals rushing toward our town!

Felix: Take cover, for raging bulls are trampling our crops! Sheep and horses are crushing every flower and bush!

Amy: (*screaming*) Thousands of locusts devour the leaves from our trees!

Phil: (*running back from the shore*) Stay away from the river, for piranhas infest the water, eating fish that we need to survive!

Crowd: Mayor! Mayor! Pay the piper, and end this madness!

(*The mayor rushes into the street in his pajamas and throws a bag of money at the pied piper.*)

Mayor: Take all of it now! Then blow your pipe and lead these monsters from this town! Go now, go!

(*Taking the money, the Pied Piper smiles and puts the flute to his lips.*)

Narrator: And with that, the pied piper put his flute to his lips, played a soft, soothing tune, and led all the bulls, sheep, horses, locusts, and piranhas to walk, fly, and swim away from Hamelin.

 THE END

GOLD!

Fluency Practice Read-Aloud Plays: Grades 5–6 Scholastic Teaching Resources

CHARACTERS

Narrator
Sam Brannan
Passerby 1
Passerby 2
Frankie
Salesclerk
Customer

SCENE ONE

Narrator: It is May in the year 1849. Sam Brannan walks through the streets of a small California town named San Francisco. He holds a bottle of gold dust in his hand.

Sam: (*He yells, holding up the bottle for all to see.*) Gold! Gold! Gold from the American River!

Passerby 1: What is he talking about?

(*Sam waves his hat with one hand and the bottle of gold dust with the other. He begins to run through the streets, yelling.*)

Sam: Gold! Gold! Gold from the American River! It's all there for the taking! Make it rich in one afternoon!

Passerby 2: Look at him, running around like crazy. "Make it rich in one day!" He's a crazy man. C-R-A-Z-Y!

Sam: (*stopping to talk to a crowd that has gathered around him*) I know it sounds outrageous, but it's true! Go see for yourselves! Just stick your hands into the river and pick up a fortune in gold . . . solid gold nuggets, lying on the bottom of the American River!

Passerby 1: (*interested*) That's it? We just stick our hands into the river and pick up gold?

Sam: Yep, that's it. Oh, and . . . you'll be needing a few supplies. Just a shovel and tin pan to hold your gold, that's all, and it'll be worth the investment. You'll be rich by the weekend, sure as my name's Sam Brannan!

Narrator: The men walk away with excitement, making plans to join the hunt for gold. Sam Brannan continues to spread the news. Within days, the town is nearly empty, as almost every man has left to find gold.

Sam: (*Waving his hat and bottle of gold, he runs through the streets.*) Gold! Gold! Gold from the American River!

SCENE TWO

Narrator: Later that May, Sam Brannan stands in a general store in New Helvetia, California.

Sam: (*to a friend*) Well, Frankie, life couldn't get any better for me, huh? My store sits right here in Sutter's Fort, smack in the middle of gold territory.

Frankie: You hit a gold mine yourself, Sam, buying out all the picks, pans, and shovels in California! Why, the only place anyone can find 'em is here in your store. Folks have to shop here, or they're out of luck.

(A customer stands at the counter with an armful of mining supplies.)

Salesclerk: *(adding up the cost of the supplies on paper)* That will be sixty-five dollars and twenty-nine cents, sir.

Customer: Sixty-five dollars, for a pick, two pans, and a shovel? Why those pans cost no more than twenty cents back home!

Salesclerk: Well, you aren't back home right now. And here in Brannan's store, these pans are fifteen dollars each.

Customer: This is robbery! *(He glares at Brannan, who strolls up to the counter.)* You thief, Brannan.

Sam: I'm no thief, Mister. I saw an opportunity, and I took it.

Customer: You mean you saw people needing supplies, and you bought every necessary item around. Now no one can find a pick, pan, or shovel in the state of California without going through you and your overpriced stores.

Sam: Say what you like, but you need my pans to mine gold. Now your order is sixty-five dollars. Are you paying . . . or putting those things back on the shelf?

(Angrily, the man takes money from his pocket and throws it on the counter. Brannan smiles and walks away, hands in his pockets.)

Narrator: Within nine weeks of calling out "Gold!" Sam Brannan's store at Sutter Fort made $36,000 from selling mining supplies. Before long, he became the first millionaire in the state of California, earning more from the California Gold Rush than any miner—and without ever digging for gold.

 THE END

Fluency Practice Read-Aloud Plays: Grades 5–6 Scholastic Teaching Resources

Volcano's Edge

CHARACTERS

Narrator	Jamie West
Mr. Maxwell	Dr. Vito
Lexie Maxwell	Dr. Wu
Dr. Eldridge	

x

Narrator: It is September 2004. Sixth-grader Lexie Maxwell and her father pull into the driveway of a science lab five miles from the base of Mount St. Helens in Washington state. Mount St. Helens is an active volcano that erupted on May 18, 1980.

Mr. Maxwell: Here we are, Lexie, at the base of Mount St. Helens! How great it is that you won that science fair competition and got to come here! Thanks for picking me as your special guest!

Lexie: Thanks for bringing me here, Dad. I can't wait to see the lab—and to get close to a real live volcano!

Fluency Practice Read-Aloud Plays: Grades 5–6 Scholastic Teaching Resources

47

(They enter the building, where a man greets them. He shakes hands with Lexie and Mr. Maxwell.)

Dr. Eldridge: Hello, Lexie. Hi, Mr. Maxwell. I'm glad you could be with us today. I think you'll be pretty excited about what you'll see here. Come meet my partners, Dr. Vito and Dr. Wu, and our assistant, Jamie West.

(Lexie, Mr. Maxwell, and Dr. Eldridge enter a room and shake hands with two scientists and their assistant.)

Dr. Eldridge: Good morning, everyone. This is Lexie Maxwell and her father. Lexie won first place in the National Middle School Science Fair this spring. Her prize was to spend a day with us, and today is that day.

Jamie West: Well, you've picked an exciting time to come. We've been tracking small earthquakes around the volcano all week. This morning, we started recording four a minute!

Dr. Eldridge: They weren't coming that often when I left last night. When did they start happening so frequently?

Dr. Vito: About thirty minutes ago. Take a look at the seismograph tape.

(The scientists hurry across the room. Dr. Eldridge picks up the edge of a long length of paper that is still churning out of a seismograph machine.)

Dr. Eldridge: Lexie, come see this. This machine is a seismograph, much like the one you made to record tremors in the earth for your science experiment. In your experiment, the tremors had to be quite large for your apparatus to record them.

Fluency Practice Read-Aloud Plays: Grades 5–6 • Scholastic Teaching Resources

Dr. Wu: The seismographs we use here are quite sensitive and can pick up even the slightest tremors. Just look at how many are happening right now!

(Lexie and Mr. Maxwell study the tape.)

Dr. Vito: We've been recording tremors from the ground around Mount St. Helens since last week. They're all small quakes. None register more than 2.0 on the Richter Scale, but they're important to track. This many quakes indicate that something big is going to happen.

Lexie: Like another eruption? I read that when Mount St. Helens erupted in 1980, scientists tracked thousands of earthquakes for two months before the big eruption.

Dr. Wu: You've done your homework, and you're right. Beginning in May, our equipment detected about 10,000 tiny earthquakes around the mountain that year. The tremors started in March.

Mr. Maxwell: 10,000! That's incredible!

Jamie West: It was. But that wasn't the most incredible part. Two months later, in May, the mountain exploded, shooting ash and gas fifteen miles up into the air. It released so much ash that the skies were filled with black clouds as far away as 250 miles!

Dr. Vito: And the tremendous flow of rock and burning hot lava wiped out that many miles of forest, crushing trees and starting fires.

Dr. Eldridge: That wasn't all the damage caused, either. The blast ripped the side off the mountain, generating the largest landslide ever recorded on earth.

Dr. Wu: By the time the volcano's damage was done, 57 people and as many as 30,000 animals that lived in those forests had died.

Dr. Vito: We're afraid something similar is going to happen soon. We're recording four tremors every minute. If it stays steady, that's more than 5,000 tremors in a day!

Lexie: What happens then? What will you do?

Dr. Vito: It's time to do something right now, Lexie. We have already put out a Volcano Alert. People who live near the volcano will need to evacuate soon. They'll need to travel to a safer location until the danger passes. If the tremors stop, we'll okay their return. If the volcano erupts, the people will be out of its path.

Lexie: There's so much to learn here. I'm so glad we got to come.

Dr. Eldridge: There's a lot more to see. Our day—and yours—has only just begun!

THE END

The Four Dragons

❁ Adapted from a Chinese Tale ❁

CHARACTERS

Narrator
Long Dragon
Pearl Dragon
Yellow Dragon
Black Dragon
Old Woman
Jade Emperor
General

Narrator:	Long, long ago, there were no rivers or lakes on earth but only the Eastern Sea, in which there lived four dragons: the Long Dragon, the Yellow Dragon, the Black Dragon, and the Pearl Dragon.
Long Dragon:	I'm restless and want to get out of the sea for a while. Let's fly to the clouds today!
Pearl Dragon:	The wind is just right for a game of hide and seek. I'll hide in the clouds, and you find me.

(*Pearl Dragon flies into a cloud and disappears while others fly about, looking for her.*)

Pearl Dragon:	(*She flies out of the cloud, into view.*) Wait! Everyone come here and look at this!
Yellow Dragon:	Well, that was a short game. You gave yourself away, Pearl Dragon!
Pearl Dragon:	(*pointing toward Earth*) I know, but look what's happening down on the earth!

Long Dragon: (*peering down from the cloud*) It looks like people are putting out fruit and cakes. How about we drop down and surprise them by joining their picnic?

Black Dragon: They aren't having a picnic; they're making an offering of some kind. See the incense they're burning and the people kneeling down? They're praying for something. With the enormous spread they're putting out, it must be something they want pretty badly!

(*Pearl Dragon flies down to the earth, hides behind a tree, and listens to an old woman's prayers.*)

Old Woman: (*She is kneeling and praying.*) Earth and Sky God, see how dry our land has become. How parched are your people and our fields! Please send rain quickly so that we can grow precious rice and feed our children.

(*Pearl Dragon flies back up to the clouds.*)

Pearl Dragon: (*pointing*) See that elderly woman down there? She prays to the Jade Emperor for rain to water the fields and make the rice grow. She prays as if the people are starving, so I assume they are having a drought!

Yellow Dragon: It must be true, for look at the barren fields, cracked and hardened from the heat of the sun! Plants cannot grow in dirt like that!

Long Dragon: Those poor people definitely need rain or they will starve to death! Let's meet with the Jade Emperor and ask him to send such nourishment to the earth.

Narrator: The four dragons flew to the Emperor's palace.

Fluency Practice Read-Aloud Plays: Grades 5–6 • Scholastic Teaching Resources

Jade Emperor:	(*Arms folded, he greets them crossly.*) I am the most powerful ruler in the heavens and on earth, in charge of all that occurs, and I don't appreciate you interrupting my daily work. Why are you here in my palace and not in the sea where you belong?
Long Dragon:	Your Majesty, the earth has had no rain in a long, long time. New crops can't grow, and the crops that have grown are withered and dying for lack of water. Please, Your Majesty, we beg you to send rain to the earth!
Jade Emperor:	(*angrily*) Are you dragons trying to tell me how to do my job? Why I should have you—
Pearl Dragon:	(*bowing down before the Jade Emperor*) We mean no harm, Your Majesty. We just happened to notice that the ground is cracked and the people are sending prayers and sacrifices to you in hopes of rainfall. We know that you, Oh Great One, can help.
Jade Emperor:	(*sighing crossly*) All right. Well, you go back to the sea and let me do my job. I'll send rain tomorrow.
Narrator:	The four dragons flew back down to the sea. The next day, they watched for signs of rain, but saw nothing. Then the next day passed and the next, without rain. This continued for quite some time.
Black Dragon:	It has been ten days, and the Jade Emperor has not kept his promise. Look! People are forced to eat weeds and tree bark to keep themselves alive! They have no water to drink and none to tend crops. These people are starving while the Jade Emperor sits in his mighty palace and ignores their situation. We have to do something.
Yellow Dragon:	The sea is vast, an endless supply of water.
Pearl Dragon:	What do you mean, Yellow Dragon?

Yellow Dragon: Why don't we take matters into our own hands . . . or our own mouths, you might say? Let's scoop up the water from our sea and spray it into the clouds so it will fall down to the earth as rain!

Long Dragon: Excellent idea!

Black Dragon: What if the Jade Emperor finds out? With his ferocious temper, he'll surely throw us in prison by sunset!

Pearl Dragon: That may happen, but we really have no choice. We must do what we can to save the people.

Long Dragon: I agree; it's a chance we'll have to take. We will never regret it, for we'll be saving hundreds of lives.

Narrator: And so, the four dragons flew back and forth from the sea to the sky, filling their mouths with water and spraying the water into the clouds. The clouds became heavy and dark and the whole sky turned gray. Then at last, the clouds gave way and rain poured down onto the earth.

(*The dragons fly back to the clouds and look down at the earth.*)

Yellow Dragon: Look! Rain seeps into the parched soil, drenching every crack and crevice! I can almost hear the earth sighing with relief!

Old Woman: (*She is raising her hands to the sky.*) Rain is falling! Rain is falling! The God of Earth and Sky has answered our prayers! Our crops and our lives will be saved!

Narrator: On the ground, the wheat stalks and sorghum stalks stood up straight as the rain nourished them. The God of the Sea heard about this and rushed to tell the Jade Emperor.

(*The God of the Sea runs to the emperor and tells him the news. Furious, the Jade Emperor pounds his fist on the arm of his chair and calls to his servants.*)

Fluency Practice Read-Aloud Plays: Grades 5–6 • Scholastic Teaching Resources

Jade Emperor:	Heavenly Generals! Take your troops and arrest those four dragons! No one makes it rain but me, the Jade Emperor! No one takes matters of the heavens or earth into their own hands! I AM THE JADE EMPEROR! I AM IN CHARGE!
General:	Where should we bring the prisoners, Your Majesty?
Jade Emperor:	Get the Mountain God and bring him to me now!

(*The Mountain God appears before the emperor.*)

Jade Emperor:	God of the Mountains, I command you to bring four mountains from any place on the land and lay them on top of each of the four defiant dragons. Plant them firmly so the dragons can never get out from under the mountains and must stay there, trapped forever.

(*The dragons crouch down, covered by the mountains.*)

Black Dragon:	I will never regret helping the people!
Yellow Dragon:	We are imprisoned here, but there is much we can do to keep helping the people!
Narrator:	And so, the four dragons turned themselves into four rivers and flowed past mountains high and valleys deep, crossing the land from west to east and emptying into the sea. To this day, they remain the four great rivers of China: the Heilongjian (Black Dragon), the Huanghe (Yellow River), the Changjiang (Yangtze or Long River), and the Zhujiang (Pearl), bringing an endless water supply to the people.

 **THE END**

Babe Didrikson Zaharias

CHARACTERS

Narrator	Woman
Bobby	Newscaster 1
Louie	Newscaster 2
Matt	Spectator 1
Babe	Spectator 2
Man	George

Narrator: In 1923, Mildred Ella Didrikson stepped up to home plate. At twelve years old, she was the best baseball player in her Texas neighborhood.

Bobby: (*yelling from the outfield*) C'mon, Mildred! Send me something I can catch!

Louie: (*to Bobby*) You won't be able to catch anything she hits. She clobbers the ball every time.

(*Mildred swings the bat and hits the ball hard, sending it sailing high over the outfield and into the woods. She throws down the bat and starts to run the bases.*)

Matt: (*From the pitcher's mound, he yells as she runs by.*) Aww, Mildred, that's another ball gone! You're gonna have to start bringin' your own baseballs if you keep losing ours.

Louie: (*laughing in the outfield*) That's FIVE homeruns for the girl, gentlemen! Five homeruns in one game.

Bobby: (*He yells as Mildred runs past him at third base.*) Babe Ruth would fall over if he saw you hit. We can't call you Mildred anymore. You are the Babe!

Fluency Practice Read-Aloud Plays: Grades 5–6 • Scholastic Teaching Resources

(The boys take off their baseball caps and hold them over their hearts in a mock ceremony as Mildred runs over home plate.)

Matt: And it's another homerun for BABE Didrikson! That's the game, boys! Let's go get ice cream! *(They throw their mitts into the air and run to home plate.)*

Babe: *(She runs off toward the center of town, shouting happily.)* I'm going to be the greatest athlete who ever lived!

Narrator: Time passes, and Babe excels in every sport she tries. Along with baseball, she stands out in diving, swimming, boxing, volleyball, bowling, billiards, skating, and bicycling. In high school, Babe leads her school basketball team to victory. With Babe on the roster, the team never loses a game.

(Babe is walking out of the school gym after a game when she is approached by several men and women.)

Man: We work for Employer's Casualty Company of Dallas. Our company has a semi-professional women's basketball team, and we want to win this year's tournament.

Woman: We've seen you play, and we want you to play on our team. We'll pay you seventy-five dollars a month.

Babe: You're going to pay me to play? You'd better believe I'm interested!

(They shake hands and walk offstage.)

Narrator: Babe's talent shines on the court, and she leads the company team to victory after victory. Inspired by Babe's exceptional talent, Employer's Casualty starts its own women's track team as well.

(After a track meet, Babe wears a medal and poses for a photograph with representatives from Employer's Casualty.)

Man:	You're an unbelievable athlete, Babe. You've earned All-American honors in basketball for three years in a row, and now you've won more events in track than I can count!
Woman:	The 1932 track championships are coming up in a few weeks. You're going to be the only one competing for our team. If you do well, Employer's Casualty will win the events, but that's not all. Your performance will qualify you for the United States Olympic Team!
Babe:	I love to compete, and I know I can win.

(Babe runs off stage. When she runs on again, she is at the championships.)

Narrator:	On the day of the qualifying championships, Babe competes in eight track events. She takes first place in the shot-put, javelin and baseball throws, the eighty-meter hurdles, and the long jump. She ties for first place in the high jump and finishes fourth in the discus throw.

(Babe tosses a javelin, jumps a hurdle, and performs the high jump.)

Newscaster 1:	*(reporting the results by radio)* This is amazing! Young Babe Didrikson has won five events and tied for first place in a sixth! She has set world records and won thirty points for her team!
Newscaster 2:	Even more amazing, Babe is the only member of her team! She, by herself, has competed against and outscored teams with dozens of players!
Newscaster 1:	The second-place team scored 22 points, which is eight less than Didrikson scored—and they had 22 team members participating!
Newscaster 2:	That's right, folks! Babe Didrikson is on her way to the Olympics, just three weeks from now!

Fluency Practice Read-Aloud Plays: Grades 5–6   Scholastic Teaching Resources

Newscaster 1:	(*interviewing Babe as she arrives at the Olympic Village in Los Angeles in July of 1932*) Babe, what are your goals for these Olympic games?
Babe:	I'm out to beat everyone in sight!
Newscaster 2:	Many of our athletes have worked all their lives to make it to the Olympic Games. Has Olympic competition been a lifelong goal for you?
Babe:	Before I was even in my teens, I knew exactly what I wanted to be when I grew up. My goal was to be the greatest athlete that ever lived. Make no mistake; I'm here to win my events at these Olympic games and I'm going to. But that's not the end of my goal; it's just the beginning.
Newscaster 1:	(*later that week, after several events*) Well, sports fans, it looks like Babe Didrikson wasn't kidding! At 21 years old, Babe is clearly one of America's best athletes! She's competed in every track event in which women athletes are allowed to participate. That's three events, and Babe has won medals in all of them! She's taking home Olympic gold in both the javelin and the 80-meter hurdles, and a silver medal in the high jump!
Babe:	I should have gotten the gold. I tied my teammate, Jean Smiley, on the high jump. We both broke the world record, but the officials said my head cleared the bar before the rest of my body. That's the way I've always done it, but this time, they said it disqualified me and gave me second place. Everybody knows I deserved first.
Newscaster 2:	What are you going to do after the Olympics, Babe?
Babe:	Anything I want!
Narrator:	For the next several years, Babe plays basketball for a traveling team. Then, she turns her attention toward tennis, bowling, and golf. A star in all three, Babe's true passion explodes on the golf course.

Babe:	(*hitting the golf ball and walking off the green*) Match that, ladies! No one stands a chance against me!
Spectator 1:	People are right when they say Babe's hard to get along with. Just listen to her brag about herself! She always has to be the center of attention, and when she gets angry, look out!
Spectator 2:	Babe Didrikson may not be sugar-sweet, but she sure has talent! That woman has dominated women's golf for the past three years! She wins everything she enters, and she's amazing to watch!
Narrator:	In 1938, Babe Didrikson marries professional wrestler George Zaharias and changes her name to Babe Didrikson Zaharias. George becomes Babe's manager as well as her husband.

(*Babe swings her club again, warming up on a golf course in 1948.*)

George:	Well, Babe, you've done it again. You're the top contender in women's golf! You've swept all the major titles!
Babe:	Don't forget that I also started the Women's Professional Golf Association and won the U.S. Open this year! (*She smiles.*) Of course, I owe you some thanks for being my manager, George.
George:	There's more to come, Babe; you can count on that.
Narrator:	There certainly was plenty more. Babe Didrikson Zaharias went on to win three U.S. Women's Open tournaments and many additional professional victories and titles in women's golf. Though she died in 1956 at the young age of 45, Babe's childhood dream came true, for she is known by many as the greatest female athlete of all time.

 THE END

On Top of the World

CHARACTERS

Narrator 1
Baltimore Jack
Janey
Matthew Henson
Narrator 2
Captain Childs
Lieutenant Robert Peary

Narrator 1:	It is the year 1878. Matthew Henson clears a table at Janey's Home Cooked Meals Café in Washington, D.C.

(*Matthew holds a tray in one hand and reaches for an empty plate. A man sitting at the table notices Matthew for the first time.*)

Baltimore Jack:	(*in a friendly, curious tone*) Aren't you a little young to be clearin' my place? (*He calls to the owner as she walks by the table.*) Hey, Janey! Are you robbing the cradle for workers these days?
Janey:	I'm not robbing any cradles, Jack, don't you worry. This boy is a fine worker and a big help to me.
Matthew Henson:	(*politely*) I'm twelve years old, sir.
Baltimore Jack:	(*smiling, he lets out a soft whistle*) All of twelve years! Why, you're nearly a man!

(*Matthew finishes clearing the table and carries the tray away.*)

Janey:	I had to take him in, Jack. Both of his parents died, and he came here with no place else to go. He's been working hard for me, in exchange for food and a clean bed.

Baltimore Jack: (*motions to Matthew as Janey walks away*) Come here and sit with me a bit. (*Matthew sits at the table.*) What's your name?

Matthew Henson: Matthew Henson, sir.

Baltimore Jack: (*shaking Matthew's hand*) I'm Jack, Baltimore Jack. I'm a sailor and have been since the first day I could stand. Ever been on the ocean, Matt?

Matthew Henson: No, sir.

Baltimore Jack: There's nothing like it. Best feeling you'll ever have, standin' on the deck of a ship, cold salty sea water sprayin' in your face, just breathing in the smell of wet ropes and caught fish. Feelin' free and set for adventure with wood bobbing under your boots and that white, frosty foam all around as the waves slap the side of the boat...

(*He inhales deeply, smiles, and leans back in his chair.*)

Matthew Henson: (*excited*) I'd sure like to see that. Tell me more!

Narrator 2: For days, Baltimore Jack visits Matthew at the restaurant, filling the young boy's mind with tales of excitement on the high seas. Before long, Matthew decides that he, too, will someday go to sea.

(*Matthew walks down to the port and approaches a huge ship.*)

Matthew Henson: (*stepping on board*) Excuse me, Captain. I hear you've been looking for a cabin boy. Are you still?

Captain Childs: I've seen you before, waiting tables at Janey's place. You're a hard worker, son. My ship, the Katie Hines, will be lucky to have you. (*He shakes Matthew's hand.*) Welcome aboard.

Narrator 1: For five years, Matthew works on the Katie Hines. Captain Childs takes special interest in Matthew and teaches him reading, mathematics, navigation, and more.

Fluency Practice Read-Aloud Plays: Grades 5–6 • Scholastic Teaching Resources

Narrator 2:	In 1883 Captain Childs dies. Matt leaves the ship and travels in search of work. At age 19, he returns to Washington. Two years pass.

(Matthew walks down to the seaport again and steps onto a ship.)

Matthew Henson:	Excuse me, Lieutenant. Folks tell me you're looking for a personal assistant. My name is Matthew Henson. I'm 21, and I'd like to work for you.
Robert Peary:	I'm Lieutenant Peary. (*shaking his hand*) Do you know how to work a ship, Matthew Henson?
Matthew Henson:	I was trained by the best, Lieutenant.
Robert Peary:	Then you're hired. I'll need you to do everything I ask, as well as you can and as fast as you can. I'm an explorer, Matthew, and I don't have time to waste. One wrong move or lazy decision on your part, and the whole crew's life could be in danger. Understand?
Matthew Henson:	Where is the expedition going, Lieutenant?
Robert Peary:	As far to the North as we can get before nature stops us. My goal is to reach the North Pole.
Matthew Henson:	The North Pole? No one's ever been to the North Pole!
Narrator 1:	Robert Peary learns quickly that Matthew Henson is more skilled than the average sailor.

(Robert Peary walks up to Matthew on the deck of the ship.)

Robert Peary:	No one told me you were so good, Henson! Why, you are by far the smartest, fastest, most skilled navigator and sailor on my ship! You can't be my assistant anymore, because that job doesn't use half your skills. I'm promoting you to full crew member. I want you with me on every expedition, from here to the North Pole!
Narrator 2:	Between 1891 and 1909, Matthew Henson accompanies Robert Peary on seven trips to the Arctic. With each trip, they travel farther and farther north before ice blocks their way.

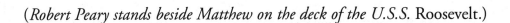

(*Robert Peary stands beside Matthew on the deck of the U.S.S.* Roosevelt.)

Robert Peary: Well, we've made it to Cape Sheridan, Canada. It's September fifth, and we're as far north as a ship can take us. As you know, nights above the Arctic circle last six months, so we won't be able to set out on foot until light returns in the spring.

Matthew Henson: I'll use the next six months to ready the equipment we'll need. We'll need to hunt musk-ox and rabbits for food, build dogsleds, and train the crew to handle the dogs.

Narrator 1:   In February, Matthew Henson and some others drive their dogsleds to Cape Columbia and set up a base camp, building igloos to sleep in and to store supplies they will need for the rest of the journey. Peary and the rest of the crew soon join them.

Robert Peary: This is it, Matthew. It's March first, and today we begin the last leg of our journey.

Matthew Henson: Everything is in order, sir. Our men, dogsleds, and gear are ready for the trek to the North Pole. Twenty-four men and 130 dogs are with us.

Robert Peary: (*shaking Matthew's hand*) I feel it in my bones that this trip will be the one, Matthew. Perhaps this time, fierce weather conditions and hardship will not send us back.

Matthew Henson: We'll make it all the way this time and be the first Americans to reach the North Pole!

Robert Peary: You realize that most of the other men in our expedition might not make it, don't you? They will give in to sickness, injury, and the dangers of the trail. But you must stay with me no matter what, for you are the only one capable. You are loyal, dependable, and hard-working. You built a house for our expedition headquarters. You learned to speak the language of the Inuit, which helped us communicate with the natives in this barren north. You've built and driven our dogsleds, trained other drivers, and learned to survive in sub-zero temperatures that would kill the average man. You are remarkable and truly the best crew member I have ever worked with.

Fluency Practice Read-Aloud Plays: Grades 5–6   Scholastic Teaching Resources

Narrator 2:	With that, Robert and Matthew set off by dogsled over the frozen ground. By April seventh, all men had turned back toward the home camp except Lieutenant Peary, Matthew Henson, and four Inuit men. These six press on, traveling what they estimate would be the remaining 174 miles to the Pole.
Narrator 1:	Along the way, Robert Peary checks his measurement tools to track their progress. Matthew Henson relies on his internal sense of direction. On the night of April sixth, by all calculations, they arrive at what they believe is the correct location.
Robert Peary:	We are very close to the North Pole. We will sleep here tonight and wait until noon tomorrow, when the sun will allow me to take exact measurements. Let's build our igloos for the night, feed our dogs, and eat dinner. Tomorrow will come quickly!
Narrator 2:	The men build igloos and crawl inside. The next morning, they step out of the igloos and into the Arctic sunshine. Then they wait until noon.
Robert Peary:	With the sun at high noon, I can see that my measurements are correct! We have reached the North Pole! We are the first Americans ever to stand here!
Narrator 1:	Lieutenant Peary cuts a narrow strip from an American flag and places it in a small tin box which he sets on the ground as a symbol of the American presence at the North Pole.
Robert Peary:	We will plant the Stars and Stripes to mark our accomplishment.
Matthew Henson:	(*standing on the flat, white ground*) At last we have reached the North Pole . . . we are standing on top of the world!

 THE END

Strike from the Sky

CHARACTERS

Narrator 1
Narrator 2
Army Private 1
Army Private 2
Lieutenant 1
Lieutenant Commander
Lieutenant 2
Radio Announcer
Civilian
News Reporter
President Franklin D. Roosevelt

Narrator 1: In December 1941, America was perched at the edge of a frightening world war. To protect the country from attack, President Franklin D. Roosevelt placed more than 100 U.S. Navy ships and many more aircraft at Pearl Harbor. This vital air base stood on the island of O'ahu, Hawaii.

Narrator 2: On Sunday, December 7, 1941, all was peaceful at Pearl Harbor. The sun rose to find sailors stretched out on their beds, catching up on sleep, reading newspapers, or relaxing on deck. All over the island, residents leisurely greeted their day off. Those at work settled in for a routine workday ahead . . . yet this day would be anything but routine.

(*Two army privates sit in an office, conducting radar surveillance.*)

Army Private 1: We've been at this radar screen a long time. Let's take one last look and then head home.

Army Private 2: Hey, what's that blob on the screen? It's huge! It looks like a whole fleet of aircraft coming our way! We'd better call Air Control.

(The phone rings in the Army's Air Control office.)

Lieutenant 1:   *(answering the phone)* Air Control here.

Army Private 1:   We're watching our radar screen, and it looks like a large group of planes is headed toward Pearl Harbor.

Lieutenant 1:   No need to worry, Private. It's probably just one of our squadrons coming back from the mainland. Good day.

Narrator 1:   Minutes later, the sound of thunder filled the sky. The Army privates jumped to their feet and raced outdoors as a massive explosion shattered the morning calm.

Army Private 2:   *(horrified at what he sees overhead)* Oh no! It wasn't our squadron at all. Those are Japanese planes in our skies. Hundreds of them. Hundreds!

Narrator 2:   From that moment on, Pearl Harbor became a scene of chaos and devastation. Bombs fell from the sky and shot through the sea waters, striking U.S. battleships and causing them to sink, burst into flames, or explode.

(A young lieutenant rushes into the office of his supervisor.)

Lieutenant Commander: What is the status, Lieutenant?

Lieutenant 2:   Thousands of men are trapped underwater in sunken ships. Thousands more are swimming for their lives, trying to escape from the water to safety somewhere.

(A radio broadcast interrupts their conversation. Both men listen.)

Radio Announcer: We interrupt this broadcast with an alert. ALL MILITARY PERSONNEL MUST REPORT FOR DUTY IMMEDIATELY!

Narrator 1:	U.S. soldiers leaped into action, setting up battle stations from ships, docks, and parking lots.
Lieutenant 2:	This is madness! The U.S.S. *Arizona* has been hit! She's exploding! Man your battle stations! Open fire!
Lieutenant 1:	The *Oklahoma*'s been hit, too! She's going down! The planes keep on coming! They're bombing our airfields and planes! They're destroying our fleet!

(*A civilian stands beside a building, with the harbor in full view.*)

Civilian:	I can't believe this is happening. What will we do? When will it stop?
Narrator 2:	Soldiers of all ranks aimed machine guns at low-flying Japanese planes.

(*An officer yells to the soldier beside him.*)

Lieutenant 2:	The last of the planes are missing their targets. The pilots must not be able to see clearly in the black smoke from all the bombing. We'll drive them out with our weapons and put an end to this air strike now.
Narrator 1:	Across the U.S., citizens listened in horror as radios broadcast first news of the attack.

(*People gather around a radio to hear the news.*)

News Reporter:	We have witnessed this morning the attack of Pearl Harbor and a severe bombing by army planes, undoubtedly Japanese. The city of Honolulu has also been attacked and considerable damage done. This battle has been going on for nearly three hours... It's no joke. It's a real war.*

Fluency Practice Read-Aloud Plays: Grades 5–6 Scholastic Teaching Resources

Narrator 2:	At 9:45 a.m., enemy planes withdrew and flew back toward their homeland. The next day, President Franklin D. Roosevelt spoke to a horrified nation.

(*People listen to the broadcast by radio.*)

President Roosevelt:	Yesterday, December 7th, 1941—a date which will live in infamy—the United States of America was suddenly and deliberately attacked by naval and air forces of the Empire of Japan. This attack. . . has caused severe damage to American naval and military forces. I regret to tell you that very many American lives have been lost. I ask that the Congress declare that since . . . Sunday, December 7th, 1941, a state of war has existed between the United States and the Japanese empire.**
Narrator 1:	So began the start of America's presence in World War II, an involvement that would last until Japan surrendered to the United States in August of 1945. It was an exhausting war and one which cost Americans dearly, both in human lives and struggle.
Narrator 2:	Today we remember Pearl Harbor and the soldiers who fought and died there. We call them American heroes.

THE END

*Portions of this text come from an actual news bulletin from Honolulu, heard over Pittsburgh's radio station WCAE, at 4:15 p.m. on December 7, 1941.

**This text is composed of excerpts from President Roosevelt's actual speech, delivered to the nation on December 8, 1941.

The Plight of Persephone

SCENE ONE

Narrator: In Greek mythology, Zeus is known as the ruler of all gods, and Demeter is the goddess of the harvest. It is said that Demeter loved flowers and plants of all kinds, yet her greatest love was for her daughter, Persephone.

Demeter: (*cuddling the infant*) Zeus, this baby girl is absolutely gorgeous! I know of no greater joy than holding her in my arms, ever close to my heart!

Zeus: She is a beautiful child, Demeter, and I'm glad you love her so much. Be careful, though, and do not forget your job as goddess of the harvest. For if you do not tend to the earth as well as to Persephone, there will be no fruits or vegetables for us or anyone else to eat and no green grass or flowers to beautify the world.

Demeter: That is the challenge of motherhood, Zeus, to give a child the love and care she needs and yet maintain my worldly responsibilities with grace and skill.

Fluency Practice Read-Aloud Plays: Grades 5–6 • Scholastic Teaching Resources

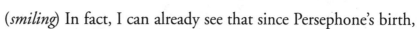

| Zeus: | (*smiling*) In fact, I can already see that since Persephone's birth, flowers appear more abundant and vibrant than ever! Surely, motherhood inspires your handiwork! |

SCENE TWO

Narrator:	Persephone grew to be a beautiful young woman. With long, flowing hair and a sweet, gentle temperament, she charmed all those who met her. Everyone who set eyes on her wanted to be by her side, even Hades, the despised ruler of the underworld.
Hades:	(*watching Persephone gather flowers in the meadow one day*) Why should I be down here alone in the underworld, in dark and drab surroundings, while such beauty walks the ground overhead? I must have Persephone as my wife!
Persephone:	(*gathering flowers*) What a beautiful day! I am fortunate to have the pleasure of gathering such a dazzling bouquet of my mother's flowers!
Hades:	(*approaching Persephone*) Persephone, come to the underworld with me, and we can rule it together.
Persephone:	(*shaking her head*) It's dark in the underworld, Hades, and there is no beauty.
Hades:	You will bring beauty just by coming there yourself, but carry your flowers, too, if you wish.
Persephone:	(*backing away from Hades*) No, but thank you kindly for the invitation, Hades.

(*Hades grows furious. Seeing the look on his face, Persephone turns to run, but Hades grabs her arm.*)

Hades: I really wasn't asking you, Persephone. If you recall, I said, 'You will bring beauty.' If you won't come with me willingly, then I shall force you down to my home.

(Persephone struggles and drops the flowers as Hades drags her down to the underworld.)

Narrator: And so Persephone disappeared from her mother's meadow. Later that afternoon, Demeter wandered the gardens and meadows, searching for Persephone.

Demeter: *(calling out)* Persephone, it will be dark soon! Bring the fragrant flowers you've gathered and put them in a vase before dinner. Persephone? Persephone, where are you?

Helios: *(calling nervously from the sky)* Demeter, I have some sad news. Hades has taken Persephone away to be his captive forever in the underworld.

Demeter: *(shocked)* How do you know this, Helios?

Helios: I saw Hades take her while I was riding my chariot across the sky and Zeus was handling some other matters. There was nothing we could do to stop Hades.

Demeter: *(angry)* NOTHING that Helios, the god of the SUN, and Zeus, the ruler of the gods, could do to stop a treacherous beast from taking my daughter prisoner?

(Zeus appears, and she turns on him.)

Demeter: Zeus! How could you let that wretched Hades take Persephone, such a beautiful ray of sunshine?

Zeus: I was busy with other matters, Demeter. I only noticed as the earth opened and I saw the last of Persephone's long hair disappear underground. By then it was too late . . . Persephone was gone.

Fluency Practice Read-Aloud Plays: Grades 5–6 Scholastic Teaching Resources

| Demeter: | (*shouting angrily*) My beautiful daughter is gone, and you did nothing to save her! My heart is broken and can never be healed, not until I see the sun shine on Persephone's face and feel her warm, loving arms wrap around me again. From this day on, I will not nourish the earth or acknowledge my duties as goddess of the harvest. The earth will be barren of all plant life—just as I am barren of my only child—and all beings on it can starve for all I care! My beautiful Persephone is gone from me, and so will all beauty be gone from the earth! |

SCENE THREE

| Narrator: | Months passed, and Demeter's words held true. The flowers of the earth shriveled and died. No tall stalks of corn swayed in the fields, no grapes grew on vines or apples on trees. For the first time ever, the world saw no harvest at all, for nothing would grow on the earth. |

(*Helios speaks to Zeus.*)

| Helios: | Zeus, you have to do something, for Demeter's broken heart has created only broken patches of dirt where hay, oats, and lilies uses to be. The people are starving, and the earth looks colorless and drab. |

| Zeus: | It is a tremendous problem, Helios, but Demeter is so distressed that she will do nothing for the earth. For as long as Persephone is gone, Demeter will not serve as goddess of the harvest! |

| Helios: | Send Hermes to bring word to Hades and talk some sense into him. |

(*Zeus motions for Hermes to come to him, and Hermes approaches.*)

| Zeus: | I need you to deliver a message. Go to the underworld and demand that Hades release Persephone. Insist that he release her into her mother's care, or I will destroy his ebony throne, seize his wealth, and see that floods, earthquakes, and other terrors destroy his underground kingdom. |

| Hermes: | (*nodding to Zeus*) Consider it done. |

(*Hermes goes down to the underworld and confronts Hades.*)

Hades: (*angry*) What do you want, message boy?

Hermes: You know my name, Hades, and you know why I'm here.

Hades: I don't think I do, for you see, I've been busy ruling the underworld with my new companion, Persephone.

(*Hades points to Persephone, who is sitting forlornly on a chair.*)

Hermes: Zeus commands you to—

Hades: My brother, Zeus, COMMANDS me?

Hermes: All right, he threatens you. Return Persephone to her mother at once, or Zeus—and all of the gods—will see you and your kingdom destroyed!

Hades: Zeus has no power over me.

Hermes: You forget, Hades, that Zeus rules all the gods. At his word, the gods of the sea, earth, and sky will join together and force you to let Persephone go. Is that what you want, to be forced out?

Hades: (*growling*) Oh, all right. (*He turns to Persephone.*) Go then, back to your mother and feast on the fruits of her world, but before you go, you must eat these pomegranate seeds.

Persephone: (*hesitantly*) Why should I eat these, Hades?

Hades: (*leaning toward her*) Because if you don't, I won't let you go . . . so eat the seeds, and be gone!

Narrator: Joyfully, Persephone swallowed several seeds and then took Hermes' hand and fled from the underworld. As Persephone left, Hades began to laugh. His laughter caused the earth to shake.

Scholastic Teaching Resources

(Above ground, Persephone and Hermes leap over cracks, trying to keep their balance as they run toward Demeter, who waits for them.)

Demeter: *(She throws her arms around Persephone.)* My daughter, my baby! Persephone! I thought I'd never see you again! *(She turns to Hermes.)* Thank you, Hermes!

Narrator: As Persephone hugged her mother, Hades began to laugh again from the underworld. The earth shook, a large crack ripped open the ground, and Hades stepped out of it.

Hades: You thought you'd never see her again, and now you think that it is I who will not see her again. But Persephone ate from the seeds of a pomegranate, an action that binds her to me forever! From now through all time, Persephone is bound to spend half of the year in the underworld. The remaining half, she may spend with you. *(Laughing, he disappears and the earth closes above him.)*

Persephone: *(consoling her mother, who weeps)* Don't worry, Mother, for at least I will be with you every spring and summer!

Demeter: *(wailing and raising her arms)* Hear me, Zeus! You have saved Persephone, but only halfway! From now on, I will be goddess of the harvest, but I shall only work when Persephone is beside me. When she is here, I will cover the world with fragrant flowers and luscious fruits. People will grow corn and wheat and eat their fill. But when the earth opens and Persephone descends to the underworld, then I, too, will go into hiding. The crops will wither and die, the grass will turn brown, and leaves will fall from the trees and render them bare. And no bud of life shall be seen until Persephone returns to me in the spring. So it shall be, for all time.

Narrator: And that is exactly what happened, which is why, some people say, that spring through fall brings beauty and harvest, and the winter months only gray, barren land.

THE END

Midnight Rescue

Fluency Practice Read-Aloud Plays: Grades 5–6   Scholastic Teaching Resources

CHARACTERS

Narrator 1
Narrator 2
Mrs. Shelley
Kate Shelley
Train Engineer

Narrator 1:   In 1881, Norah Shelley lived with her four children in a cabin not far from the Des Moines River in Boone County, Iowa. The Shelley family had little money and had suffered tragedies three years earlier: the death of the children's father in a railroad accident, and the death of the fourth child, Michael, who had drowned that same year.

Narrator 2:   Norah Shelley, broken in spirit and health from enduring such loss, struggled to raise her family alone, with the help of her eldest child, Kate.

Narrator 1:   In 1881, Kate was fifteen years old, a hardworking, compassionate young woman who spent her time plowing the family's fields, tending the cow, hogs, and chickens, and helping to care for her brother and sisters. All the while, Kate tried to maintain her own schooling, with the hope of someday becoming a teacher.

Narrator 2:   In July of that year, something happened that would transform Kate from local teen to Iowa heroine.

(*Kate is outside with her mother, taking sheets off the clothesline.*)

Mrs. Shelley: (*looking at the sky*) The sky is getting dark, with such black, heavy clouds! A storm's coming, and it looks to be a big one. I don't know how much more rain we can take. Honey Creek is already up to its banks with all the rain we've had this month.

Kate: I can feel the wind picking up. Maybe I should round up the animals and put them in the barn, to be safe.

Mrs. Shelley: (*resting her arms on the laundry basket she carries and smiling a tired smile at Kate*) Thank you, Kate. I don't know what I'd do without you. (*She calls to the other children, who are playing in the yard.*) Margaret, Mayme, John! Time to get inside!

Narrator 1:   That night, Kate and her mother stood at the window.

Mrs. Shelley: This storm is ferocious! I haven't seen wind this hard or rain this heavy in years.

Kate: Mother, look! When the sky lights up again, look toward the barn! Honey Creek has flooded its banks! The water is going to flood the barn!

Narrator 2:   Kate hurriedly pulled on a coat and rushed out into the storm. She waded through mud and water to the stable and let the animals out to run free.

Kate: Run to high ground, where you will be safe!

(*Mrs. Shelley opens the cabin door for Kate, who dashes back inside.*)

Kate: You know what Father always said about heavy, prolonged rains and the railroad! The bridge over Honey Creek is only as strong as the soil it stands on. With this storm, that soil is washing away, and you know what that means—

Narrator 1:	Just then, Kate and her mother heard a heart-wrenching sound—the hiss of a steam engine followed by the horrifying crash of metal.
Kate:	(*screaming*) The bridge is out! A train's gone down! (*She and her mother look at the clock and then back at each other.*) AND IT'S ELEVEN O'CLOCK, ALMOST TIME FOR THE MIDNIGHT EXPRESS!
Narrator 2:	Kate knew that every night at midnight, a high-speed train traveled over the high railroad bridge above the Des Moines River and then across the smaller railroad bridge over Honey Creek, directly in front of the Shelley home.

(*Kate pulls on her coat again and prepares to go outside.*)

Mrs. Shelley:	(*alarmed*) What are you doing?
Kate:	I have to warn someone to stop the Midnight Express!
Mrs. Shelley:	Kate, you'll risk your life out there!
Kate:	The Midnight Express carries 200 people. I can't let it go off the bridge!
Mrs. Shelley:	Go then, and do what you can.
Narrator 1:	Kate lit a lantern, kissed her mother good-bye, and rushed outside. Wading up to her knees on flooded ground, she made her way to the broken bridge.
Narrator 2:	Huge flashes of lightning revealed two men below. Of the four who had ridden the small engine, two were still alive, clinging to tree limbs in the raging creek. One saw Kate's light and called out.

Fluency Practice Read-Aloud Plays: Grades 5–6   Scholastic Teaching Resources

Engineer:	(*screaming*) Run for help! Tell the stationmaster he must stop the Midnight Express!
Narrator 1:	Kate jumped off the broken bridge and sunk to her ankles in mud. Struggling against the storm, she forced her way to the Des Moines Bridge, the only pathway to the station.
Narrator 2:	Kate held her breath and took several steps out onto the long, steep trestle. She shook with fear as a streak of lightning revealed trees, bushes, chicken coops, and boards swept along in the wild current.
Kate:	(*crying out and dropping to her hands and knees*) The wind is blowing so hard, and this bridge is so high; I am sure to fall! (*Kate bows her head against the wind and closes her eyes in fear.*) But I must keep going. Two hundred lives depend on me. I can't let that train go down!
Narrator 1:	Kate began to crawl on her hands and knees. She lost her balance, and the lantern smashed against the bridge and dropped into the churning waters below. In the deep, frightening blackness, Kate clung to the cold steel rails, groping from one railroad tie to the next, painfully guiding herself across the endless trestle. Repeatedly, her skirt caught on protruding nails and spikes. Her hands and knees scraped across rough, splintered wood, and rain drenched her body.
Kate:	(*Crawling onto soil, she touches the ground with surprise and relief.*) At last, I've reached solid ground!
Narrator 2:	With renewed energy, Kate stood and raced down the track toward the station. Bursting inside, Kate called out to the stationmaster.
Kate:	You must stop the train! The bridge at Honey Creek is out, and a train has already fallen off!

(Kate puts a hand to her head and faints, dropping to the floor.)

Narrator 1:　　At once, the station sounded a long, loud emergency whistle, calling for help, and commanded the Midnight Express to stop. Townspeople readied a small steam engine with ropes, shovels, and other rescue gear.

Kate:　　*(She is regaining consciousness.)* Wait, take me with you!

Narrator 2:　　With Kate's help, the rescue party saved the two surviving engineers. Then they brought Kate home where she fell into bed, exhausted.

Narrator 1:　　While Kate slept, news of her heroic deed spread across the nation. By morning, reporters swarmed to the Shelley home, asking questions and wanting photographs of Kate, Honey Creek, and both bridges.

Narrator 2:　　From that day on, Kate was a national heroine. Passengers, railroad workers, townspeople, and representatives from the State of Iowa gave Kate medals, free passes, money, flour, coal, and other gifts to show their appreciation. Admirers from coast to coast sent Kate letters and wrote poems, stories, and books to tell her tale.

Narrator 1:　　Kate Shelley died in 1912, but her bravery has never been forgotten. The bridge she once crawled across has been replaced with a newer, steel version. Today, it is the tallest railroad bridge in the United States and is named in her honor, the Kate Shelley Bridge.

❄ THE END ❄

Fluency Practice Read-Aloud Plays: Grades 5–6 • Scholastic Teaching Resources